What Readers Are Saying About *Agile Coaching*

This book provides clear, proven advice that will be helpful to any Agile coach or ScrumMaster. From starting the transition to keeping the code clean to running a retrospective, this book covers what you need to know to help you get the best out of any Agile team.

▶ **Mike Cohn**
Author of *User Stories Applied* and *Agile Estimating & Planning*

I've seen numerous presentations about being an Agile coach, and none of them comes even close to the kind of practical advice Rachel and Liz have packed into this printed nugget of gold.

▶ **Lasse Koskela**
Coach, Reaktor Innovations, and author of *Test Driven*

Writing a good book about coaching is an extremely difficult task. Rachel and Liz have done a great job explaining why you can't have prescriptive, well-defined steps to coaching teams (there is no silver bullet. . . not yet!). Every team is composed of different individuals, and they all operate in very different contexts. The beauty of this book is it makes you "think" rather than blindly follow. It demonstrates through examples how, as a coach, one can be agile and pragmatic about Agile adoption.

▶ **Naresh Jain**
Agile Software Community of India

The authors share their wealth of experience with the reader. This book is packed full of hints, tips, ideas, and inspiration for helping you help an Agile team. Unlike many other books, this one discusses the rough edges, corner cases, and difficult bits that most teams face.

▶ **Allan Kelly**
Author of *Changing Software Development: Learning to Become Agile*

I once started to write a collection of patterns for building a beautiful company. The collection included a pattern called "The Right Coach" with the following observation: "A coach is like a mirror. You could dress yourself without a mirror, but you'd risk not getting it right." Coaching is important—both for growing companies and for growing teams. Since Agile teams have started forming, we've seen the need for coaching, but we've been missing the guidebook, the "coach" for the coach! So, I'm delighted to say that the book is here. This helpful manual is right on target with the kind of practical advice you would expect from two seasoned coaches and authors. If you are interested in coaching, have worked with a coach, or are just thinking about what that experience would be like, this book should be in your hands.

▶ **Linda Rising**
Coauthor of *Fearless Change: Patterns for Introducing New Ideas*

This book is an essential guide to all those seeking to become an effective software coach. Rachel and Liz wonderfully capture the essence, spirit, and best practices of coaching Agile teams.

▶ **Xavier Quesada-Allue**
Agile coach and author of the Visual Management Blog

Coaching an Agile team is difficult in the best of circumstances and, for a newer coach, can be intimidating. Every day presents new situations where the team will look to you for expertise, and every day presents new challenges that need to be gently addressed before they turn into real problems. *Agile Coaching* guides readers through a vast set of circumstances. Drawing on their years of experience, Rachel and Liz give new coaches the confidence they need while teaching us old dogs some new tricks.

▶ **Russ Rufer**
Silicon Valley Patterns Group

This book gives an excellent overview of Agile coaching and very practical tips on how to help teams start applying the most common Agile practices. It's a must-read for all Agile coaches and ScrumMasters.

▶ **Kati Vilkki**
Manager, Agile Coaching, Nokia Siemens Networks

Agile Coaching

Agile Coaching

Rachel Davies

Liz Sedley

The Pragmatic Bookshelf
Raleigh, North Carolina   Dallas, Texas

Our Pragmatic courses, workshops, and other products can help you and your team create better software and have more fun. For more information, as well as the latest Pragmatic titles, please visit us at

http://www.pragprog.com

Printed in the United States of America.

ISBN-10: 1-934356-43-3
ISBN-13: 978-1-934356-43-2
Printed on acid-free paper.
P1.0 printing, July 2009
Version: 2009-7-20

Contents

Foreword

If you're interested in Agile software development or in software development at all, chances are that Rachel and Liz's book will help you. It's not just about coaching; it is about playing the game well.

When we are really serious about something, whether it's golfing, playing the piano, painting, or just trimming down a few inches, we often benefit from the help of a coach. A good coach knows the subject material and can assess where we stand and what will help us improve. The coach can help us stay motivated when we reach the inevitable plateaus in progress.

Most of us spend more time at our work than we do in an avocation like golf or sit-ups. Yet all too often we get little or no help in improving. It turns out that opportunities to help others, to be helped, and to help ourselves are all around us. This book will help each of us find those opportunities and capitalize on them.

Agile software development is deceptively simple. At its core, it's just a matter of choosing some things to build, building them over a short period of time, thinking about what has gone on, and repeating the process until our product is ready to go. Nothing to it, right?

It turns out that there is a lot to it. Most teams who start using Agile methods see benefits very early on. The very best Agile teams, however, see their productivity double—or more. These high-performance teams may not be all that much smarter than your team, just working in better ways. Each team needs to find better ways that work for them, and that's what this book is really about: finding better ways and getting them in place.

If you're an itinerant Agile coach, this book will help you serve your clients better. If you're an internal coach, a ScrumMaster, or a customer/product owner, this book will help you serve your team. If you're "just" a team member, this book will help you too, because there are small coaching opportunities in front of us all.

Rachel and Liz take us through all the key aspects of the Agile cycle, from forming a team, estimating, and planning to tracking and demonstrating to holding the retrospectives that help us improve. They help us figure out how to improve our definition of "done" and how to test and build our software so as to get done more quickly. They help us understand the importance of clean code and how to get it.

Now, software development is quite rich and complex, and teamwork is as well. It's impossible to put everything we need to know into one book, or even a dozen. What Rachel and Liz do for us is identify important aspects of our team's process and give us some key ideas that will help us understand and shape our practice. In every chapter, they list the hurdles we're likely to encounter as we try to grow and a checklist of some key things to be aware of.

Rachel and Liz also give us examples from their own long experience helping teams. There's something about a real story that makes things clear to us, and it's freeing to know that someone else has been in a similar situation and has survived. Once we know there are ways of dealing with a problem, we can calm down and start making good choices.

The stories, checklists, and hurdles are alone worth the price of the book. But wait, there's more. Rachel and Liz also give us some good advice for improving ourselves, in their *Growing You* chapter. One bit of advice from that chapter is to read one book per month about our profession. My advice is to start with this one. You'll be glad you did.

Ron Jeffries (www.XProgramming.com)
July 2009

Introduction

Agile is all about teams working together to produce great software. As an Agile coach, you can help your team go from first steps to running with Agile to unleashing their full Agile potential.

This book is all about how to enable teams to get the best from Agile. It focuses on practical advice, tips, and techniques for coaching teams to improve their effectiveness. It's for anyone who wants to coach their team in Agile development—whether you are a project manager, you are a technical lead, or you are simply working in a software team.

The art of Agile coaching is understanding the situation, the values underlying Agile software development, and how the two can combine. As an Agile coach, you don't need to have all the answers; it takes time and a few experiments to hit on the right approach. We've worked with teams who've come up with great solutions, and we learn from every team we work with.

We will be talking you through the whole spectrum of Agile practices from creating plans to deploying software. We've chosen to explore a wider set of practices than in some agile methods, including both planning and technical, because they work together in a reinforcing system. However, in our experience, the hard part is not the mechanics of Agile practices but how to coach people in adopting them. That's what this book is about.

Generic Agile

Most teams we work with are using a mixture of Extreme Programming (XP), Lean, and Scrum, so throughout the book, we will refer to this as *Agile*.

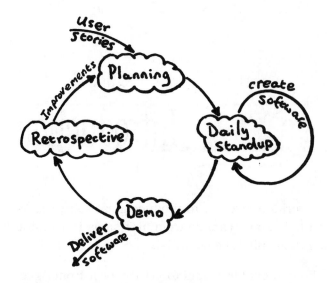

A simplified life cycle for this Agile process is shown here. It shows that a team works in iterations to deliver software. Each iteration opens with *planning* based on *user stories* and closes with a *demo* and *retrospective*. The team works in a shared workspace and starts their day with a *daily standup* around their *team board*. Software is created using *Test-Driven Development* and *Continuous Integration*. Some teams work in short one-week iterations, while others work to a monthly cadence.

As Agile coaches, we work to establish a healthy collaboration between a cross-functional development team and their business stakeholders. We use the term *customer* for the business representative who works with the team (equivalent to a product owner in Scrum) without going into responsibilities of team roles, which in our experience vary from one organization to another.

The life cycle shows how these Agile practices join up. But you don't have to start implementing Agile from the top. Your team could get started with any practice in this cycle and then fold in more practices over time.

The Aim of This Book

Coaching is all about working with people. These people work on projects and in teams, and these teams are within an organization. Every person, project, team, and organization is different, so we can't prescribe exactly what you should do in your situation.

Rachel Says...

Showing, Not Telling

I don't think it's possible to talk purely about coaching without getting into how Agile practices work. It's one of the main things we do as Agile coaches. You're there to help the team—to demystify, to remove confusion, to make what was difficult easy.

Imagine if you found someone using a hammer to bang in a nail, but they were using the handle to hit the nail. You'd offer to show them how, and then you'd turn it around and hit the nail with the hammer head. Now they know how to use the hammer, their job becomes easier, and they're happier using the hammer because they understand how it works.

I often meet teams that are trying to follow Agile practices, but what they're doing is quite odd and not a good use of their time. I show them how they could do things differently rather than telling them what they should do. They choose whether to apply what I've shown them.

Instead, we give general guidelines to follow and ideas on different options you can apply.

We can't give you formulas to follow that will always work, because no two situations are alike. Depending on team context, we might give opposite advice to one team than another. For example, we would normally recommend that the project manager attends the daily standup, but there have been times when we've recommended that he doesn't. Some factors to bear in mind are team size, pressures on the team, and experience of team members.

Throughout the book, We share stories about what we did in different circumstances, along with some more specific tips that you can use if your situation happens to match the one we describe. You'll need to decide whether to apply our advice to your teams.

Time and experience are necessary to become an effective Agile coach. Reading this book will add to your knowledge. It will help you avoid coaching pitfalls and provide you with tips to improve your coaching. It will give you inspiration and ideas to apply what you learn with your team.

How to Read This Book

Each chapter is relatively self-contained. Feel free to dip in or read the book sequentially. We start with discussing general coaching principles and then move on to how to apply them to coaching specific Agile practices. Take the time at the end of each chapter to review the checklist and reflect on how you could apply what you've read with your team.

We've encountered many hurdles that we had to overcome when coaching Agile teams. We'll share these at the end of each chapter together with our advice on how to clear them. They're not meant to be an exhaustive list, but we hope they'll give you some inspiration if you get stuck.

Acknowledgments

This book would not have been possible without the support of our families. We wrote much of the book over weekends and evenings and had many long Skype calls while they tip-toed around waiting for us. So, thank you to both our families for everything: Don, Alex, Abby, and Josh, and also Ian, Sapphire, and Stephanie.

We'd like to thank our official reviewers: Mike Cohn, Frank Goovaerts, Ben Hogan, Leigh Jenkinson, Colin Jones, Allan Kelly, Turner King, Simon Kirk, Lasse Koskela, Andy Palmer, Timo Punkka, Xavier Quesada-Allue, Dan Rough, Russ Rufer, Karl Scotland, Bas Vodde, Leah Welty-Rieger, Matt Wynne, and the Silicon Valley Patterns Group.

We'd also like to thank the following people who have reviewed parts of this book to help us improve it: Esther Derby, Willem van den Ende, Ellen Gottesdiener, Julian Higman, Ron Jeffries, Norm Kerth, Antony Marcano, Richard Lyon, Ivan Moore, Linda Rising, Jerry Weinberg, and Rebecca Wirfs-Brock.

Thanks also to Ron Jeffries, Michael Feathers, Lasse Koskela, Antony Marcano, Ivan Moore, and Karl Scotland for their written contributions to the book.

Finally, we want to thank Andy Hunt, Dave Thomas, and Jackie Carter from Pragmatic Bookshelf, especially our editor, Jackie, who patiently coached us over the past year and helped us pare down our writing to extract the essence. Thank you for your support.

Part I

Coaching Basics

A journey of a thousand miles begins with a single step.
► Lao-tzu, 604BC–531BC

Chapter 1

Starting the Journey

Let's get started on your journey to becoming an Agile coach. Your mission is to help teams produce great software by applying Agile. To succeed, you'll need passion and enthusiasm for Agile. Experience applying Agile is also required before you can guide a team in it.

Your first question is probably, "What does an Agile coach do?" quickly followed by "How can I do that?" Your success, as an Agile coach, boils down to learning basic coaching skills and strategies that help you work with people to implement change.

We'll get into how to coach teams in specific Agile practices, such as Test-Driven Development and user stories, later in the book. Before that, let's run through what Agile coaches do and how they do it. Then we'll cover some useful preparation to help you put your best foot forward.

1.1 What Does an Agile Coach Do?

Your goal is to grow a productive Agile team that thinks for itself rather than relying on you to lay down the Agile law. Showing people how to be Agile isn't enough; they need to change how they work and how they think in order for Agile to stick. They often need to unlearn old habits before they can work effectively as members of an Agile team. As an Agile coach, your job is to guide them through the rough patches until they can find their own way.

Each team is different, made up of a unique cast of characters with their own project challenges. That means how you coach a team depends on what they need from you. If a team is new to Agile, then you'll be like a sports coach, actively showing them how Agile practices work. For more experienced teams, you'll be more like a life coach, listening and asking questions that help them improve rather than offering solutions.

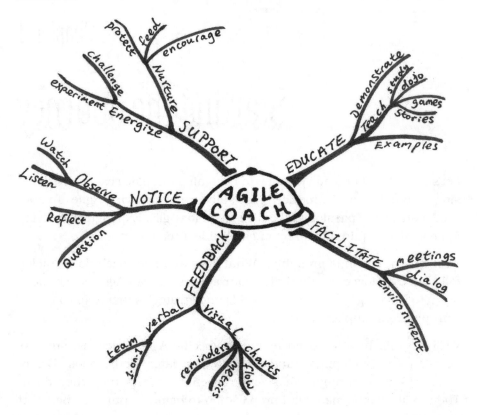

This mindmap gives you an overview of what's involved. Let's explore each branch to see some of the things you will be doing:

Notice: Keep your eyes and ears open, notice how the team works, and then reflect on underlying causes.

Feedback: Give feedback about what you noticed to the team. Help them incorporate feedback into the way they work so they spot problems themselves.

Educate: Look for ways to encourage learning. You can do this by demonstrating how to be Agile, by telling stories, and by running training sessions.

Facilitate: Make it easy to be Agile by smoothing the path for constructive communication and collaboration.

Support: Be there when the team gets stuck, encourage them to keep going, and help them stay energized.

That might seem like a lot, but you don't need to do all these things at once. Coaches work one step at a time rather than creating a whirlwind of change. You'll find that the secret to success all comes down to developing the right attitude.

1.2 Developing a Coaching Attitude

Developing a positive attitude to your coaching is essential. You have to believe change is possible before you can make it happen. You need to show you're open to new possibilities and ideas while keeping your feet firmly on the ground. What a team needs from you is guidance on what they can do and a shot of courage to make these changes a reality.

Here are some important habits to develop as an Agile coach:

- Lead by example.

- Keep your balance.

- Set a realistic pace.

- Mind your language.

- Learn as you go.

Let's look at each of these in turn to see what they mean in practical terms.

Lead by Example

Give the team a real-life example by following Agile principles yourself. For instance, an important principle of Agile is to work at a sustainable pace (rather than getting burned out). So, make sure you leave the office at a sensible time to demonstrate that you take this principle seriously. Have conversations face-to-face instead of sending emails to demonstrate how to communicate. Try making a list of the principles that you would like to demonstrate and how you will do so.

Following your own advice is a powerful way to lead the team. When you're consistent with your own recommendations, people know they can rely on you. Take a moment now to think about ways you can show that you practice what you preach.

Keep Your Balance

It's natural for the team to react against changes, and as a coach, you're often the one who's introducing change. Expect some backlash with every change, and don't let the team's reaction throw you off balance. They may simply be recovering from the last "great idea from management," which didn't work out, and be cynical about making any change at the moment.

Never take criticism personally; it's most likely change rather than you that the team is reacting to. Stay positive, and keep your coach's hat firmly in place. Take some positive action, such as working out the root causes of any team gripes, and then look for ways you can resolve them.

Set a Realistic Pace

Patience is one of the most important qualities of a coach. Don't expect instant perfection from the team; change takes time. Take care not to add to the stress on the team by finding fault with their early attempts to be Agile or having unrealistic expectations. Remember, the team may be under other pressures that are distracting them from learning about Agile right now. Chill out, and don't add to the pressure.

When the team is slow to apply what you've been teaching them, don't jump to blame them. Take responsibility, and look to yourself for the cause. Are you going too fast? Have you chosen a bad time to get started? Back off for a while, and let off some steam by talking to someone outside the team.

Patience is not the same as complacency—don't give up. You do want to see a change eventually, so keep pushing gently and persistently. Can you find another way to help the team see how important it is to slow down and learn these new Agile skills? Look for ways you can support the team by getting the rocks out of the way and making it feel safe to try something new.

Mind Your Language

This might be a surprise, but when you're a coach, you have to watch your language! Of course, it helps to keep it clean, but what we're driving at is that you need to take care how you talk to the team.

Show that you are part of the team by talking from a team perspective using "our"/"we"/"us" rather than "I"/"you"/"they." Say, "We need to update our release burnup chart," instead of "You need to update your release burnup chart." The difference is quite subtle but important because it shows the team you're on their side. You don't need to use inclusive language all the time; when sharing a personal opinion, it's clearer if you use "I," as in, "I've noticed that our tests are taking more than an hour to run."

If you notice something unusual, say so. For example, "I haven't seen it done this way before," or the more concrete, "The last team I worked with checked with their customer before they put out a release." Sharing this as information rather than advice or criticism can lead the team into considering alternative approaches.

Avoid making sweeping generalizations. Don't use words like "never," "always," "right," and "wrong," because doing so can discount the situation at hand. Try hard not to dismiss past practice by saying it was wrong or incorrect; this creates bad feeling, and people may feel they've lost face.

Beware of putting people in boxes by using labels and talking about "the developers" or "management." Putting people in categories creates a barrier to communication. Try to use people's names.

Learn as You Go

When things don't go as you were hoping, don't panic. Take time to reflect on what happened and why. The most powerful lessons are learned from mistakes. Ask yourself what you can do differently if you're faced with the same situation again.

Although it's tempting, don't try to protect the team from making mistakes. Instead, give the team room to make mistakes, and be there to help them learn from the experience.

You don't need to be busy working with the team all the time. Take time to stock up on fresh ideas, and keep up with what's happening in the Agile community outside the company. Read books, read blogs, listen to podcasts, and try to connect with others who are interested in Agile. We'll talk more about how to develop yourself in Chapter 14, *Growing You*, on page 199.

1.3 Getting Ready to Coach

Like a sports coach, an Agile coach needs to know how to play the game. You need to understand how Agile works and get some experience applying Agile in practice. When you have experience as an Agile practitioner, you'll have a better appreciation of how it works, and you can use real examples to illustrate your points.

Practice explaining Agile.

Experience using Agile doesn't automatically make you good at explaining Agile techniques to others. Get some practice in, and learn how to field unexpected questions. Find someone who is willing to listen who doesn't already know what Agile is about. If you can't find anyone at work, if your family are now Agile experts, and even if your cat is sick of hearing about Agile, try going to your local Agile user group to hear how other people do this. You can pick up some tips from the pros by listening to Agile podcasts; a good place to start is the Agile Toolkit.[1]

Before you start working with the team, do some groundwork to get clear about your role. Being Agile is not an end in itself. What benefits do you want to bring to this team? What is expected of you by both the team and their managers? Take the time to answer the questions we've listed in the sidebar on the next page. These can help you work out how best to be introduced.

Arrange to be Introduced

Starting off on the right foot is important. Before you can do any coaching, you'll need to be introduced to the team. Even if you already know the team members, they need to understand your new role as Agile coach.

No Formal Introduction

Henry was brought in as an Agile coach to help a team adopt Test-Driven Development, but he didn't get introduced as a coach. He assumed that the development manager had already explained his role to the team. But when he started trying to provide advice to the team, he met a lot of resistance.

In the eyes of the developers, Henry was "the new tester" whose job was to write automated story tests for them. They didn't see any reason to listen

---

1. See http://agiletoolkit.libsyn.com/.

Exercise: Questions to Ask Before Coaching

Here are some questions that are useful to try to answer before you start coaching a team.

Motivation:

- Why am I coaching this team?
- What difference do I want to make?
- What do I want to learn?

Skills:

- What do I have to offer?
- What do people need to know about me?
- How will I make this information available to the team?

Responsibilities:

- Do I need to get anyone's agreement to start coaching?
- What are the responsibilities of my official role?
- Do any of these conflict with being an Agile coach?
- How will I review my progress?
- How will I know when I'm done?

Support:

- What support can I get from others?
- How will I be introduced to the team?
- Are there other Agile coaches I need to work with?
- Do I need to communicate progress with coaching to a sponsor?

to him and saw his attempts to give them feedback on their process as unnecessary and interfering. This situation was very frustrating for Henry and quite difficult to resolve after this bad start, because the team was now used to ignoring him.

Being introduced properly helps build credibility and trust with the team, which is essential before they'll listen to you. They need to understand what you can offer them and what support you have from management. Remember also that if they're new to Agile, they may also need some overview about what Agile is and the benefits of it in order to make sense of your role.

Who does the introducing depends on your situation:

External coach:

If you're being brought in as an Agile expert to help the team improve, then talk to your sponsor to arrange an introduction. Help them make a powerful introduction by making sure they know what credentials will be relevant to mention to the team. For example, he could mention you're a contributor to an open source testing tool, that you're a prolific blogger, or that you worked on a groundbreaking Agile project at another company. This comes across much better than saying, "I'd like you to meet, Allan. He's an Agile guru."

Internal coach:

If you have been asked by your manager to be a coach on a pilot project or to support a wider rollout of Agile in your organization, then your team needs to know about your new role. They also need to hear more about the plans for the Agile transition. Arrange for a senior manager with some authority to explain the drivers for Agile in your organization. This shows the team that you have blessing from management and makes it more likely that the team will pay attention to your recommendations.

Extending your role:

It may be that no one has asked you to introduce Agile, you believe Agile will give your team an edge, and you have the authority to extend your role to become an Agile coach. You don't have anyone to introduce you, but don't be tempted to skip an introduction. Set up a session with the team to introduce your new role and to answer their initial questions about moving to Agile.

Introductions are a two-way thing. An introduction gives you an opportunity to get to know the people on the team. They may be worried that you have a hidden agenda. Talk to them openly about your motivation to take on the role of an Agile coach. Show that you're on their side by asking them about their hopes and fears for the project. This should give you some good ideas about what you can do next to support them and earn their trust.

After your introduction, spend time with the team getting to know the players and seeing how they work. Sit with the team rather than observing them from afar. Try to blend in like a chameleon; otherwise, the team puts on its best behavior whenever you're around.

Figure 1.1: PROpER COACHING CYCLE

The team needs to build confidence in your ability and experience before they'll be willing to follow your lead. It can help to start with something that grabs their interest, like running an interactive session to learn about Agile, such as the XP game[2] or a coding dojo.[3]

1.4 How to Start Coaching

You're probably itching to get started, but where do you get started? There's no right place. The simplest approach is to pick one thing and jump in. If it's not obvious what problem to work on first, then you can take an Agile approach. Brainstorm a list of problem areas to work on that could improve life on the project for the team. Then prioritize this list based on your coaching mission—now you have a starting point.

You can apply our PrOpER cycle (illustrated in Figure 1.1) to each coaching episode.

Problem: Pick a problem to work on. Watch how the team works. What needs to be improved?

Options: Consider your options. What could you try that might influence the situation for the better? List at least three options.

Experiment: Pick one option to try.

Review: Review the outcome. Did you improve things? Even if things haven't improved, have you learned something?

---

2. See http://www.xp.be/xpgame.html.
3. See the sidebar on page 141.

Let's work through an example together.

Problem: Jack arrived late for the daily standup meeting today. It happened last week too. You're concerned because he's working on building a new test environment. He's missing important information about problems the team is finding with the current test environment.

Options: Here are a few options that you might consider:

Take the bull by the horns: When Jack arrives, ask for some time to catch him up on what he missed at the daily standup. While you're going through those issues, talk to him about the importance of attending the whole daily standup.

Educate the team: Run a training session for the whole team to learn how to improve their daily standup; this may help Jack understand why it's important for everyone on the team to attend the meeting.[4]

Leave them holding the baby: You need someone to cover for you; ask Jack whether he can help you out by running the daily standup tomorrow.

Wait and see: Do nothing, and wait to see whether the team lets Jack know his lateness is a problem by themselves.

Experiment: You choose the first option—to talk to Jack about it. Approach the conversation by mentioning that you noticed he's missed the daily standup a couple of times. He seems genuinely surprised that this matters; from his perspective, he's not working on any of the customer's stories, so surely he doesn't need to be there. Explain the reason for your concern is that he's missing information from his teammates that needs to be considered in building the new test environment. Also explain that the daily standup is for the team, not the customer. Suggest that he call a meeting with the tester to go through the issues he missed. He nods and agrees to be on time for the daily standup tomorrow.

Review: Review the outcome. The next day, does Jack arrive on time? Did your conversation make a difference? If there's still a problem, then what other options can you try?

---

4. Bill Wake's "Scrum from Hell" is a role-play exercise that might work well here; see http://xp123.com/g4p/0410b/index.htm.

Rachel Says...

Rewind and Fast-Forward

It's important to have a sense of time, as a coach, to think about cause and effect. When you notice something, use your imagination to rewind or fast-forward events.

Finding out more about what happened in the past can make you more aware of what obstacles might crop up in the future. Ask the team, "How did things get this way?"

Think things through when making changes. What are the longer-term consequences of current actions? What might happen if things continue the way they are?

When trying to come up with options, here are some ideas to consider:

- Surface the problem: Make the problem visible to the team.

- Socialize the problem: Talk with the team about the problem.

- Wait and see: Leave this problem; if it gets worse, the team will probably notice.

- Go sideways: Sell the problem to someone else inside or outside the team.

- Root cause analysis: Look for the root cause of the problem.

- Educate the team: Provide the team with more information so they see a solution.

- Put them in charge: Hand over responsibility to the team or a team member.

We've talked about how you use the PrOpER cycle on your own, but it doesn't have to be a secret. You can also use the PrOpER cycle openly with the team, informally or in a retrospective.

1.5 Maintaining the Pace

Creating Agile teams takes time, and some days it seems like you're making no headway. There's sure to be setbacks along the way that can make us feel like giving up. So, how do you maintain momentum and keep on going?

James Shore gave an inspiring talk, "Change Your Organization (For Peons)," about his experiences trying to introduce Agile techniques into his organization (see *Proceedings of the 2003 Agile Development Conference* [Lit03]). We like his advice about finding small pleasures. He says, "Organizational change is largely outside of your control. Find small things at work that you can do every day and that give you a feeling of satisfaction."

If things seem to be going slowly, don't feel bad; try to make one small step forward every day. James found that even though people did not make a change in how they worked at first, he was slowly able to change how people thought about things. This mental shift in the team was invisible, so it felt like he was making no progress. But explaining the ideas was a necessary step before they started putting Agile into practice, which his organization eventually did.

A Shoulder to Cry On
by Rachel

On my first big engagement as an Agile coach, I was one of a number of external Agile coaches brought in to help teams make a transition to Agile. It was a tough environment to start in. I was used to working with developers who liked being Agile and were keen to do more of it. But these teams were not so enthusiastic, for good reasons—the change was being rushed, and they didn't like it.

What helped, in the face of this resistance, is that the coaches linked up to work together. Quite a few of us knew each other from Extreme Tuesday Club in London.[5] When I hit a roadblock with my team, I'd go and find one of the other coaches. They might have already solved a similar problem, and that might save us some time. But even if they hadn't, it helped to compare notes and talk it through with them. It also helped to have someone to commiserate and have a cup of tea with when the going got tough.

---

5. Extreme Tuesday Club is an Agile user group that has been meeting in a pub in London every Tuesday since 1999—http://www.xpdeveloper.net/—and is where Rachel and Liz met.

Try to find other coaches inside or outside the organization who you can connect up with and form your own mini-support network.

We find it's also useful, if you get stuck, to think about what another coach we know might do when faced with the same situation. Look for opportunities to work with other Agile coaches; you'll likely notice they have different coaching styles. Watch how they handle situations to expand your coaching repertoire. Rather than mimic exactly what they do, which is likely to feel uncomfortable, consider how you might be able to absorb some of their techniques into your own approach.

Breaking In Your Coach's Boots

We found that it took time to get comfortable being Agile coaches to make the shift to giving advice rather than playing an active role in getting the work done. At first, you may find it strange being less hands-on and letting the team decide rather than setting direction yourself.

In *Becoming a Manager* [Hil], Linda Hill follows nineteen new managers through their first year as managers. She illustrates how hard it is to shift roles. If you were a tech lead or project manager and are now an Agile coach, it will take time to shed your old identity at work and take on a new one. So much of our life revolves around our work and how we define ourselves that changing our job title creates ripples everywhere.

You may prefer to make the shift gradually by starting as a "player-coach." When you take on the role of coach as a player on the team, you'll have the advantage of experiencing problems with the way the team works directly rather than by observation. The team knows that you appreciate problems from firsthand experience, and they respect you as their peer.

We find that if we're heavily involved with project tasks, it's hard to get time to coach the team. When we play the coach role from the sidelines rather than playing on the field, we can focus completely on improving process and team work. You'll find that playing the coach from this position helps you see the big picture so you're in a better position to help the team optimize the whole.

So, how can you tell how you're doing as an Agile coach?

- Looking back, is the team more Agile now than it was a month ago?

- Have you had a positive influence on the team?

Liz Says. . .

Credit the Team

Don't expect to get recognition for your work as an Agile coach. It's a supporting role rather than one that delivers direct benefits.

A good coach gives credit to the team. When you work on an idea with Frank, it's Frank's idea if it succeeds, and if it doesn't, then commiserate together.

- Review your answers to the preparation questions in the sidebar on page 9.

Another sign that the team has absorbed your coaching is that you'll hear team members give out advice based on what you've explained previously. The joy of coaching has to be when you see the team achieve their goals without consciously trying to be Agile. They're not plodding along; there's an energetic buzz as the team swarms around the work.

Moving On

What happens to a cucumber if it stays in a jar of brine for too long? It becomes a pickle—whether it wants to or not. In *The Secrets of Consulting* [Wei85], Jerry Weinberg warns us about "getting pickled"—if we stay with the same team (or even the same company) for more than a few months, we can lose our fresh perspective. You stop noticing problems that once jumped out at you. You start to absorb the same mind-set as the rest of the company and find yourself saying, "That's just how it's done around here."

If you're concerned that you are getting pickled, try explaining the team's process and the challenges that you are facing to an outsider. As you explain it, you might start to see (again) the hiccups in the process, the hidden assumptions, and the elephants in the room.

Just when life seems good on the team, notice your job as coach is probably done. The team has become self-coaching, and you need to break their dependency on you for the answers. It's time to move on!

1.6 Hurdles

Here are some hurdles you may encounter.

No Time to Coach

If you are heavily loaded with project work and people in the organization rely on you as the only person who can get specific tasks done, you will not have the bandwidth to take on a coach role. You don't have to give up your desire to move into a coaching role. Instead, make a plan to extract yourself from being the person everyone depends on. Slow down, and show other people how to do the key tasks they rely on you for.

Consider switching into a different team that can give you opportunities to get some Agile experience that you can build on. However, if the source of the stress is you and your internal drive to take too much work on, take a break to get some perspective on the current situation.

No Experience

When you meet a situation that is outside your experience on Agile teams, be open about that to the team rather than bluffing. For instance, you may have plenty of experience with small projects but haven't worked on a large, distributed Agile project yet. Or perhaps you don't have any recent experience in programming, and you recognize that the team needs help getting started with automated testing.

An Agile coach doesn't need to have all the answers; it's sometimes better if you don't. Not being an expert can help you stay detached enough from a problem that you can still see it from an outside perspective.

Help the team work through the issue by facilitating the discussion and by researching what other Agile teams are trying inside your organization or outside. Experience reports from Agile conferences can be a useful source of ideas. Agile user groups are also another great place to find out what other teams are doing. If you think that the team needs specialist help, explore the possibilities of bringing in an expert to guide the team through the challenge it faces.

Blockers to Agile

There are times we meet teams that face serious roadblocks to becoming Agile. We recommend you address these before you attempt to coach a team in Agile. Otherwise, it can be a frustrating experience for all involved, and problems caused by not establishing the right starting conditions can cause people to blame Agile for the failures.

Sometimes the blockers are technical, and other times they're organizational. For example, if a team isn't using source control, they are at risk of losing changes to the software. They need to install this basic development practice before making a start with Agile practices.

When a company is in the middle of a reorganization, then people are more focused on keeping their jobs rather than becoming Agile. We would advise against coaching while this is going on because the pressure on the team will be too distracting, and you'll probably be wasting your time.

1.7 Checklist

- Practice explaining Agile to others. You can do this with anyone willing to listen. Agile user groups are a good place to refine your Agile pitch.

- Do some groundwork, and work out the best way to be introduced to the team.

- Find ways to show that you apply Agile principles yourself. For example, you can work iteratively and have face-to-face conversations rather than asking questions by email.

- Apply the PrOpER cycle to your coaching interventions. Start with the problem, consider at least three different options that you can take, pick one and try that as an experiment, and then review the outcome.

- Pause to reflect and learn from your mistakes. Leave room for the team to learn from mistakes too.

- Look for opportunities to learn from other Agile coaches, both inside and outside your company.

- If you work with one organization for a long time, you can get pickled. When the team is running an effective Agile process, it's probably time to move on.

Chapter 2

Working with People

To help Agile teams improve, you need to work with the individuals in the team. They're the number-one experts on how they work and why. Tap into their expertise to reveal what's holding them back. Listen to their concerns and ideas one-on-one to give you insights on how they can improve. Give them feedback to help them see where they can improve.

Agile throws a team into closer collaboration than they may have experienced at work before. As you'd expect, when people work closely together, conflicting opinions come to the surface. Coach the team to explore these differences, and find solutions that everyone can live with.

This chapter is all about skills that will help you work with people on the team. We'll start with the art of listening, and then you'll learn how to give feedback that hits the spot. Next we'll run through techniques that can help you resolve conflicts and build agreement on the team.

2.1 Listening

A man goes into a doctor's office and says, "Doctor, Doctor, it hurts when I raise my arm over my head." The doctor replies, "Then don't raise your arm over your head!" It's not a great joke, but Doctor, Doctor jokes have a common theme: the doctor isn't really listening and doesn't help solve the problem. As coaches, we don't want to fall into the same trap.

A coach listens deeply. We listen to the troubles and woes of the team. We also listen for the germ of an idea that needs support to take shape.

Yes, I'm Listening

Listening is an interactive process. If you're wearing a stony-faced expression, a speaker can't tell whether you're really listening. Give them some signals that you're listening and want to hear more.

Here are some tips that help you put someone at ease so they feel comfortable to open up and tell you the whole story:

Create space: Don't chime in and talk about yourself. If there's a pause in the conversation, you don't have to fill the void.

Be open: Put on a relaxed and open expression rather than frowning or grinning, which might make them feel you're judging them or not taking them seriously.

Show interest: Use your eyes, look into their face, and make eye contact from time to time (without staring intently) to show you're interested in what they're saying.

Affirm: Nod your head to show you understand. You can also make "mmm" and "ah" sounds to show you heard them.

Respectful listening shows that you care about the person who is talking, which in turn has an effect on how much they will listen to you. Prove you really did listen by following up afterward.

Listening well is a skill that you can learn. Start by giving your full attention to the speaker. Stop what you are doing, and turn to face them. If they appear hesitant, suggest moving out of the team workspace to find somewhere quiet to sit or go out for a coffee; this can help open up the conversation because they don't need to worry about being overheard and because there are fewer distractions.

Give them your full attention, and keep it with them rather than glancing at your watch or checking your cell phone. Now show you're listening by following the tips in the sidebar on the current page.

Listen before giving advice.

We find the hardest part of listening is resisting the temptation to jump in too early with advice or to switch the conversation to a similar story that happened to you. Focus on the person who's talking, and try to understand the feelings and needs that underlie their words without judging.

When Chris says, "Nicola ignored my design," mentally unpack this as Chris holds the opinion that Nicola ignored his design. You may have a different view of what happened, but now is not the time to share it. Take the time to listen to Chris's story properly before checking into the facts. As the conversation unwinds, pause to check that you understood what was said by paraphrasing what you heard: "So, what I'm hearing from you is that you provided a design, but for some reason Nicola has not implemented it."

If the pace of the conversation allows, ask clarifying questions to draw the story out without taking sides. Pick your questions carefully so

Ask clarifying questions.

that it's clear you are clarifying rather than challenging or criticizing their actions. You could ask, "When did you notice that Nicola had not followed the design?" or "Have you talked to Nicola about this?"

Reading Between the Lines

People usually speak much slower than you can think, which is why it is so hard to give your full attention when someone else is talking. Don't spend your time mentally building your response, because this can divert you from listening. Use the time to examine the whole situation.

Focus on the person speaking, notice how they express themselves, and consider their possible motivation for starting the conversation:

- Are they looking to gain support, provide a favor, or repay a favor?

- Are they looking for empathy, advice, or more information?

- Are they flagging a problem because they want you to help them solve it?

Pay attention to any nonverbal cues such as body language and the tone of voice they use:

- Are they upset, angry, excited?

- Do they seem uncomfortable or relaxed about the conversation?

- Are they acting a little different than usual?

Don't assume lack of eye contact is a sign that they are hiding something; people often look away when they are trying to remember something or feeling uncomfortable.

Put yourself in their shoes—imagine how they feel about the situation, and empathize by summarizing. You could say, "Chris, it sounds like you're feeling frustrated. You worked over the weekend to get that design finished, and now your work has not been used." This helps show the person that you are listening and also gives them the opportunity to correct you and continue their story.

Maintaining Trust

In closing a conversation, summarize the key points you heard, and check them with the speaker. Do you understand their needs?

The speaker had a reason for wanting to share information with you, and they may not do so again if you do not follow up the conversation. If a problem has been disclosed, you'll want to do some further investigation before committing to a course of action, so don't feel obliged to make any immediate promises about resolution.

Finally, to maintain trust, it's important not to betray confidences. Check whether the person prefers what was discussed to remain private or whether their concerns should be shared with the team and, if so, how to approach this.

Background Listening

Besides listening in the context of a one-to-one conversation, you will also be involved in many team conversations. Most of the same rules apply. When facilitating a meeting, pay attention to each speaker, and wait until they have finished speaking before asking clarifying questions. It can also help to paraphrase what you heard them say to check that you understood and make it clear for everyone else in the meeting.

When you participate in a team conversation rather than running a meeting, you still need to listen carefully to the words being used and watch the body language of the team. If someone makes a statement that strikes you as indicating that they have misunderstood something, such as "Now that we're Agile, we don't need to document the release," you have a choice, You could pause the meeting and check group understanding about that point, without singling out the person, or you can address the issue after the meeting. We find it helps to capture a mini-quote—taking note of the exact words used in your notebook—as a reminder to follow up.

Listen to the level of conversation in the team outside meetings too. A healthy team buzzes with sporadic conversation throughout the day because team members are truly working together to create software together, whereas a quiet team may not be working as a team at all.

Liz Says...

Don't Abuse the Power of the Pen

If you are writing up notes on the board in a meeting, beware of filtering what you heard. Make sure that you write all the points mentioned rather than only those you agree with. If people don't feel that they've been heard, they are likely to stop contributing to the conversation.

Some filtering of trivial comments is necessary. However, take care to use words people said rather than put words in their mouth. Don't be afraid to ask them if you have captured their point accurately.

Listening to the team provides you with a wealth of information about them and the issues they are struggling with. Deep listening also shows that you care about their concerns and are interested in helping them. It puts you in a better position to influence the team by giving them feedback.

2.2 Giving Feedback

When you notice behavior that is not working well for the team or an individual, you naturally want to help them to see what needs to change. You want to share your observations, in the hope that you will influence them to change their behavior, but it can be hard to know the best way to get your message across. For example, if a team member has been acting disrespectfully, how can you bring it to their attention in a way that they will listen to you? Let's take a look at how to give the team feedback.

Your first step in providing feedback is to separate the basic information (what you saw or heard) from your assessment and feelings about the situation. Talk about the data from your perspective, and give specific examples of what you saw and heard rather than your interpretation. If you can give this information sooner rather than later, it will be easier for the person to remember what they did and why. For example, when you say, "Nicola, I noticed that you kept having to step out of our meeting yesterday to take calls on your cell phone," it summarizes your observation. Follow this by saying something like "I am concerned that you missed Chris's walkthrough of the design he's been working on," which sums up your feelings and assessment of the situation.

Now it's their turn. Listen to their experience of the events. Maybe there's a good reason for their actions that you don't know about yet. Nicola may be getting calls from day care about her sick child, or she may be getting requests for help from her previous project team. She may be unaware she missed anything important, or she may have already taken time to catch up with Chris after the meeting.

If you still think there's room for improvement, make some suggestions of how they might handle similar situations in the future. Ask for their ideas too. Then you can talk through the pros and cons of each option. For instance, if a customer often arrives unprepared for planning meetings, this can waste the team's time. You could suggest that they block out a time buffer between meetings rather than rushing from one meeting to the next. You could offer to work with them on their preparation next time. Or they could arrange a session with the team lead to prepare for planning.

Give specific examples of what you saw and heard.

If you want to give positive feedback, you don't have to phrase it as a judgment and rate their achievement as in "Fantastic job!"— a light touch works better. Let them know you noticed what they did and the positive effects that resulted. For example, "Mike, I noticed that the build is running a lot faster since you reconfigured it. Yesterday, it flagged up a broken test in a couple of minutes so Jules was able to fix the problem before getting started on a new task."

Timely feedback helps nudge the team into improving their process without directing them what to do. As the team starts to benefit from process changes, they usually become more reflective on how they are working together and accept feedback from each other more readily.

Sometimes you will want to give feedback that hasn't been asked for. Take care in doing this, because the person you want to offer feedback to may feel like you are stepping out of line and criticizing them. If you state feedback too bluntly, you can upset them so much that your message does not sink in or they feel alienated by what you said. Slow down, and start by asking for permission to share your feedback with them. Now work through the previous steps.

Rachel Says...

<u>**Catch Them Doing It Right**</u>

Encourage the team when they're learning new skills, such as Test-Driven Development, and aren't sure if they're on the right track. Take time to notice what the people on the team have done well by giving them positive feedback.

Catching someone doing something right also has an effect on you, as the person giving the feedback. You're probably unaware of it, but human beings process the world by categorizing. We sort people based on what we see of their actions, which is usually not the whole story. Linda Rising, in her talk "Who Do You Trust?" at the Agile 2008 conference, suggested that when you catch someone doing it right, you're categorizing that person as a winner rather than a loser in your own eyes. This helps you see their other actions in a positive light.

What if they've also not done such a great job on something? Just because you noticed, you don't have to say anything. When I'm tempted to criticize, I try very hard to keep my mouth shut.

2.3 Resolving Conflicts

As a coach, you may be drawn into situations where there is a conflict within the team that's holding them back. Sometimes this is an open disagreement, and other times it's a festering situation where there's a disagreement, but it's not openly discussed. If you detect that there's a concealed conflict within the team, spend time listening to the concerns of individuals on the team. This helps you understand the causes before surfacing the conflict with the team.

Before you dive into the role of peacemaker, consider whether the dispute will resolve itself without your help. If you intervene every time there's a dispute, then you may find team members start whining to you, as if you were a parent being called upon to resolve squabbles between kids.

Nonviolent Communication

Marshall Rosenberg teaches an approach in *Nonviolent Communication* (Ros03) that is a useful technique to apply to diffuse conflict. The basic principle is that you ask about the feelings and needs of others. By listening to them, you help build enough trust that others will listen to you. The four basic steps are as follows:

- Observation: When you. . . (describe your observation)?
- Feeling: Are you feeling. . . (guess the emotion)?
- Need: Because you need. . . (guess the need)?
- Request: Would you like (me, him, her, them) to (specific action)?

For example, "When you walked out of the design review, I guess you were feeling frustrated because you needed more time to explain your new design to Roger. Would you like me to arrange a follow-up meeting with Roger so you have some time to get your idea across?"

When you are acting as a mediator, be clear that in this role you can't take sides. Listen to the problem from each side, and demonstrate that you understand what is being said by restating the problem in your own words (or ask them to restate each other's problem). Next, try to detach the problem from the individuals and frame this in the context of the team. Explain the situational factors that you see at play in the situation—such as if there's pressure on the team to deliver and people have been working late. It may even be useful to create a diagram of effects to explore the forces involved.

Resolving disputes within the team helps stop them from working at cross purposes. However, remember that some differences in opinion are healthy. Too much emphasis on peace and harmony within the team can signal that the team members are complacent. *Groupthink* [Jan82] can set in—where the team favors group happiness and conformity over critical thinking. Whenever making important decisions, try to make sure the team considers different options. Ask the team for a devil's advocate perspective to anticipate problems with what they're proposing to do.

2.4 Building Agreement

When you introduce new practices, it helps to find out whether you have buy-in from everyone on the team. Some team members may be enthusiastic about the changes, but there are likely to be skeptics too. One technique that helps reveal differences of opinion is gradients of agreement, which we learned from *Facilitator's Guide to Participatory Decision-Making* [KLT+96].

Rather than asking team members for a simple yes or no vote on a proposed action, you can create a gradient scale that runs from Endorse to Block. Draw this up on a flip chart, and ask everyone in the team to indicate their level of support with a check mark. This allows you to distinguish a whole-hearted yes from a lukewarm one and a strong no from a mild one.

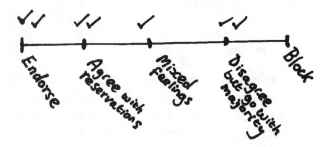

Using a gradient scale enables you to show when there's a lack of consensus. Consensus is important because when a person does not agree with an action, they are unlikely to implement it enthusiastically. Sometimes you may decide that it's worth going ahead without consensus, framing a change as a timeboxed experiment that the team reevaluates at the next retrospective. But if the scale reveals a lot of negative opinion, try to work out a new solution that everyone on the team can live with.

Using Gradients of Agreement
by Rachel

I used gradients of agreement in a workshop about a team's approach to testing. I knew from pair programming with developers on the team that they did not all have the same passion about writing automated unit tests. A couple of the developers were keen to install a CI server to run tests automatically after every check-in. I was concerned that this didn't have the full support of the team; in fact, the team didn't have a set of tests that could be run by any developer yet. I drew up a gradient chart and listed the following alternative goals. Then I asked the team to vote.

- A. Automated tests should be run every day.

- B. Automated tests should be run manually before every check-in.

- C. Automated tests should be run automatically after every check-in.

Everyone on the team indicated strong support for option A. However, the votes on options B and C were mixed and showed there was not enough support to try these yet. We talked through some of their concerns, which mostly centered on the time automated tests would take to run. However, the team did have consensus on option A, so the remainder of the meeting was spent working out what the team needed to do to establish a daily build and test routine.

By using gradients of agreement, I was able to focus the team on the option with the most support, and the team avoided wasting time installing software that the majority of them were not ready for yet. It took another couple of months before the team was ready to get started with using a CI server to run tests automatically.

Use this technique to establish the level of agreement amongst the team. If you don't have a place to draw up a gradient chart, then you can use *fist-to-five* voting as an alternative to a written gradient, where holding up a fist indicates a block and the number of fingers indicates a level of support from one to five. Whatever method you use to uncover a disagreement, take it seriously, and explore the concerns behind it.

2.5 Hurdles

The following are some hurdles you may encounter.

Emotional Outburst in a Meeting

If someone has an emotional outburst because of a conflict in a meeting, we recommend you call a break to give them time to calm down and recover their composure. Before you resume the meeting, take a moment to talk to the person to understand what has upset them. If you decide to continue the meeting, don't pretend nothing happened. Acknowledge that feelings are running high, and check with the whole team whether they can continue with the meeting or whether the issue that caused the upset should be resolved first.

 **Liz Says...**

Don't Put People in Boxes

There are many models out there that can be used to categorize people into levels or types. Models can be useful to help you determine how best to present information to the team. A great one to start with is the Dreyfus learning model, which Andy Hunt explains in *Pragmatic Thinking and Learning: Refactor Your Wetware* (Hun08).

These are some of the other models to learn about:

- Myers-Briggs types*
- Thomas-Kilmann conflict modes†

Watch out that you don't get too carried away with applying any one model; this can get in the way of appreciating that each person is unique and different. Learning about more than one of these models helps you see the same behavior through different lenses, giving you a better way to evaluate people's actions.

---

*. See http://www.myersbriggs.org/.
†. See http://www.kilmann.com/conflict.html.

Lack of People Skills

Often you find that people have been drawn to a career in software development because they prefer working on their own and find interacting with people difficult. Be aware that people have different communication preferences. You may need to be more direct with some people and give others more space.

Cultural Differences

In different cultures, different things are considered polite. For example, Liz is from New Zealand, and some English people find the way she phrases things to be too direct. You may find that people who've grown up in a different culture than you say "yes" to mean "I'm listening," rather than to mean "Yes, I know how do that." Some cultures are more comfortable with a meritocracy, which tends to be a working assumption for Agile teams, whereas other cultures prefer a distinct hierarchy.

Help your team become more attuned to cultural differences such as tolerance for ambiguity and individualism. One way to approach this is to explore the work of Geert Hofstede on cultural dimensions with the team.[1]

2.6 Checklist

- Practice deep listening to understand the problems the team faces and build trust. Give your full attention to the person talking, and ask clarifying questions to check that you have understood what they are saying.

- When giving feedback, separate what you saw or heard from your feelings about the situation. Give specific examples of what you noticed rather than general comments. Tell them what you saw or heard, and then ask about their explanation of events. Now put your heads together to come up with ideas for handling the situation next time.

- If a conflict erupts, make sure all sides get to share their viewpoint. Don't step in to resolve every conflict for the team because otherwise they rely on you as a peacemaker rather than learning to get along.

- Use gradients of agreement to reveal the level of support for a change. This allows the team to find out whether there is major or only minor disagreements.

---

1. http://www.geert-hofstede.com/

To improve, people must first learn new ways of doing things.
► Guiding principle

Chapter 3

Leading Change

Sometimes you'll be introducing new Agile practices; other times you'll be helping a team fine-tune its process. Either way, you need to lead the team to make changes. It's not as simple as telling people what they need to do. People need to understand what's driving a change before they'll throw energy into it.

So, how can you open their eyes to new possibilities? Start slow; give them some time to think about change before pressing them into action. Look for opportunities for them to learn about Agile. Then engage them in designing change by asking questions and building on their ideas.

3.1 Introducing Change

Start advocating Agile techniques to the team, and you'll soon find that people raise objections. Even when there's a compelling reason to change, it's natural to be concerned about the risks. Assure them that it's safe to become more Agile. Tell them stories about other Agile teams you have worked with to give them an appreciation of what's possible.

Show your confidence in the ability of the team to change. Your belief in their success can give them courage to take the first step. Talk about "When we..." rather than "If we...," and then make sure they know you're there to provide support and help them keep going.

Take care not to push a team into making changes too quickly. Allow time for new ideas to soak in. The team needs time to talk through a change before starting to implement it. This gives them a chance to think through the implications and to understand how they can adjust what they do now.

Rachel Says...
Agile Is Not a Religion

Beware of becoming an Agile zealot, because this can backfire and put people off. Don't treat people who are not applying Agile as fools who just need to see the light! This is disrespectful, and people simply won't listen to your rants.

You need to build bridges to help people see how these strange new principles could work in their world. You can even enlist the help of someone who is skeptical to help you find holes in your proposals.

No One Listens to Me

Richard was a senior developer who would suggest lots of great process improvement ideas to his team. But telling people his idea was as far as he went with it. Months later the team often implemented something he'd originally suggested. Then he'd grumble, "I suggested that ages ago! Why doesn't anyone listen to me?"

What he didn't realize is that you have to do more than suggest a course of action for people to follow it. You need to lead the way by explaining why it's important and then show them how to get started with it.

The other thing he missed is that people were listening to him because they did implement his ideas eventually. It just took time to build up enough support on the team to try it.

Show Them How

It's not enough to convince the team that change needs to happen; you also need to show them how to get started. Suppose you suggest to a team that writing unit tests will help them reduce defects. Don't be surprised if everyone nods and agrees but no one actually starts to write tests. They need support to implement this change; use the PrOpER cycle (Section 1.4, *How to Start Coaching*, on page 11) to work this problem through.

Rachel Says...
Be Open

Some coaching techniques we read about could be labeled "manipulative." For instance, you might deliberately make a mistake to draw in the person who you're working with to correct it. I prefer to avoid such ploys and be transparent about what I'm doing. A different way of encouraging someone to do the same thing is to say, "Now that I've written a few story tests, it's your turn."

Here are some options to try:

Educate the team: Arrange an in-house training course so they can learn how to write unit tests.

Demonstrate: Pair with developers to show them how to write unit tests.

Make it visible: Work with the team to agree on a goal for how many unit tests they will write every day; track progress toward this goal on the team board.

Sell the Problem

As a coach, you'll see lots of opportunities for improvement. Before you share your ideas, be prepared to sell the problem that's driving the change. Paint a clear picture of the likely outcome if the team doesn't make changes. For instance, you could say, "Right now code gets handed back for bug fixing, which delays the release. We're disappointing our customers when we miss delivery dates. They're already under pressure from management to outsource this work. If we put out another release that crashes and loses all the transactions, we're toast."

There's no need to lay it on too thick; you don't want to make the problems sound too difficult to overcome. You simply want everyone to be clear why not making a change is a problem.

Leveraging Resistance

Dale Emery has written an excellent article called "Resistance as a Resource" (Eme01). In it, he talks about the types of resistance you are likely to encounter and how to respond.

Dale urges us to "stop thinking of people's responses as resistance." Instead, think of each response as information that you can learn from.

When people bring up objections and reasons not to change, listen carefully to them. Try to understand their viewpoint. Can you agree with them on some things? Acknowledge their concerns—a change may indeed take more time, cost more money, or be hard to do. Explain why, despite all that, you still think it is a good idea, and the benefit will outweigh the cost. For example, refactoring code before every check-in *will* mean it takes longer to implement each user story, but it will also mean that the code remains easy to maintain over the longer term.

You can sell a problem more convincingly if you can point to supporting evidence. Your prediction will be powerful in the previous example if you can share some data on how often code has been bounced back to developers to fix bugs before it could be released. However, take extra care not to criticize the team for the way they work now. As a coach, your focus is process improvement, not individual performance.

Building Ownership for Change

Once you've sold the problems, it's time to focus on solutions. Encourage the team members to look at the positive outcomes of improving their Agile process. Build shared ownership by talking through the pros and cons of making changes.

Let them know the options you see, and invite them to share their ideas. How would they like to work? Do they see opportunities for improving their career prospects and building better products? People are more likely to follow through when it's *their* idea.

These process improvement conversations become a regular part of life on the team once they start holding retrospectives. One approach to adopting Agile we've used with some teams is to make *retrospectives* the first Agile practice to introduce. Retrospectives provide the team

Liz Says. . .

Pick Your Battles

Ideally, you can see dozens of problems and opportunities for improvement. But if you talk about all the problems you see, you will come across as negative, and people will soon stop listening to you.

You need to make an impact for people to follow your lead. Kent Beck puts it like this: "Begin with small changes. Do one thing now and everything else later" (from *Extreme Leadership* (Bec00)). So, pick only one problem to work on with the team, and focus your efforts on solving it.

with a forum to discuss problems and fold in changes every few weeks (find out more in Chapter 13, *Driving Change with Retrospectives*, on page 183).

Make Change an Experiment

When you encounter resistance, propose trying something different as an experiment. Framing a change as an experiment helps focus the team on the benefit because you'll need to discuss how to evaluate whether the experiment is a success. If they can measure an improvement, this gives the team a reason to continue.

We'll let you in on a secret: once a team takes the plunge and tries a change as an experiment, team members get used to the new way of working. Now, making the change back to the original way of working is the change that they hesitate over. You'll also notice that each change they adopt reduces their resistance to the next change. So, start the team off making some small changes, such as redesigning the workspace or introducing a regular team lunch, to get them ready for bigger changes.

3.2 Asking Questions

Another way you can lead the team to consider change is simply to ask questions. When you ask someone a question, you show that you respect their opinion and you're interested in their answer. They need to engage their brain to come up with an answer. When they do so, they join your quest to improve how the team works. A thought-provoking question may even lead them to follow up on your conversation and take action.

Here are some powerful questions you can ask:

- What could we do to stop this bug from happening again?

- How can we ship on time?

- How can we work more effectively?

Challenge assumptions. Often people are held back by self-imposed beliefs. You can use questions to challenge their beliefs about how the organization works and what they can and cannot do. For instance, what's stopping them from doing what they know the right thing is? If you get an answer like "Management won't let us," then probe for more information. Which manager? How do they know that manager won't let them? Help them see that they've made assumptions that haven't been verified.

Are Rules Really Rules?
by Rachel

Sometimes a team justifies not trying a change because of company policy. It's worth checking whether that policy really is a rule.

One team I worked with had a process improvement group that worked in another office. The process improvement group provided a set of document templates on its intranet site. The team believed that they were required to use these templates, which was the reason they gave for not being able to try user stories.

I picked up the phone to the process improvement group and asked them whether using the templates was mandatory. The surprising answer was that the templates were just provided as examples based on documents from another project. There was no requirement to use the templates!

How should you ask questions? Don't ask closed questions that generate a yes/no answer or basic information. Instead, ask open questions like "How?" and "What would happen?" to open up the conversation and invite the person to reflect and share their opinion.

> **Ask open-ended questions.**

Take care about using "why" questions, because they can sound like you're criticizing when you don't mean to do so. For example, "Why did you do that?" sounds accusing, whereas "What were you trying to do?" sounds friendlier. "Why" questions tend to be about the problem, rather than about the solution. Focusing on what needs to happen to improve is more pragmatic than dwelling on what went wrong.

Ask questions only when you're genuinely interested in their answer. If you nod in approval, this implies you're looking for a particular answer, which can come across as patronizing. So if you're looking for a particular answer, don't start the conversation with a question.

What to Ask

There are many different types of questions. The following are some useful questions that you can try.

Ask for Help

One way to engage the team in change is to come right out and ask for their help—not in a general way at a team meeting but one-to-one over coffee. Share a problem you are facing with them, and ask for their help. They may help by offering ideas, support, or something more practical. Most people love to help and will be flattered that you asked them.

Thinking Questions

Remember, it has to be the team doing the thinking about the issue, not you. You can facilitate their thinking by asking *thinking questions*.

David Rock claims in *Quiet Leadership: Six Steps to Transforming Performance at Work* [Roc06] that the most powerful question you can ask when coaching someone who comes to you with a problem has the word *think* (or a similar word) in it, such as the following:

- How long have you been *thinking* about this problem?

- How often do you *think* about this?

- Are you satisfied with the amount of *thought* you have given this problem?

- Can you spot any gaps in your *thinking*?

- What *insights* are you having?

Thinking questions encourage the person to make a mental shift and think about the problem at a more strategic level. When you ask a thinking question, it helps them step out of the details of the problem and look at it from a different perspective. Keep in mind, though, that thinking questions may not work if a person is stressed or emotional, because they may be too distracted to distance themselves from the problem.

Reflective Questions

Encourage the team to notice more about how they work by asking questions about what they noticed afterward. Suppose you want to increase awareness of how their daily standup varies so you can ask afterward what they noticed during the meeting. You can simply ask, "What did you notice about the daily standup today?" Or you could dig deeper by asking some follow-on questions like these: How did the meeting flow? Did people update tasks on the team board? How was the meeting today compared with yesterday?

Share your own observations to help them understand what kind of thing you're interested in. For example, I noticed there were less interruptions today and the meeting seemed to flow better. I was wondering if that was because Yuan was dialing in from home and we had to pass a cell phone around to talk to her. It seemed we were using the phone as a speaking token. Maybe we should try a speaking token for our daily standup when she's back?

Five Whys

Five Whys is a technique, invented by Taiichi Ohno [Ohn88], that you can use with the team to do root cause analysis. When applying Five Whys, make sure you explain what you're doing—that you are applying a technique rather than repeating the same question because you are unhappy with the answer.

Start by asking about the surface problem. Come up with a solution for that, and then dig down further by asking what caused the surface problem, what caused that, and what caused that. By the time you have asked "Why?" five times, you should reach the real problem that will be a system problem—such as making unrealistic promises to customers or not investing in training for the team.

Here's an example:

Why 1: "Why didn't we put the software live yesterday?"

"We had too many open defects."

Why 2: "Why do we have so many open defects?"

"Because when the testers find them, they just enter them into bug-tracking software and don't tell the developers."

Why 3: "Why don't the testers tell the developers?"

"Because the developers are busy working on something else."

Why 4: "Why don't the testers and developers work together?"

"Because the testers have to be available to all teams, not just this team."

Bingo! This is the system problem that is stopping the team from shipping. This is the problem that requires a change in approach. If the team can get a dedicated tester to their team, rather than having a pool of testers for the whole company, bugs would get found quicker and get fixed quicker, giving them a better chance of shipping on time.

Why 5: "Why don't we have enough testers so that every team can have their own tester?"

"Because we can't afford any more testers."

And so we find out that one of the reasons why the team didn't ship yesterday was because the company doesn't value testers enough to hire them.

The Five Whys is a powerful technique; however, it can expose problems that are outside the control of the team and have to be escalated to the right level in the organization.

When Not to Ask Questions

Take care not to ask questions when you actually want to give guidance. If you ask a question, you have to accept the answer, even if you disagree with it, and this makes it harder to give the advice you wanted to give. For example, if you ask, "How could you have found this bug earlier?" and they respond "By doing more manual testing," then it makes it harder to guide them toward automated testing because it can feel like you're correcting them.

If all you ever do is ask questions, it can seem like you're holding out and not sharing what you know. This can make people doubt that you are genuine, and they may not be open with you. Bear in mind that a question can sound like you're picking fault if the other person doesn't believe you care about the answer. They may think you are poking your nose into something that is not your business and clam up.

Feeling Manipulated
by Liz

Once I had a project manager who was unhappy with a decision I'd made to not fix a bug. Rather than come out and say he was unhappy with me, he asked, "Don't you want people to think the project was successful?" His loaded question made me angry, because he was trying to manipulate me to do what he wanted, rather than trying to understand my rationale. I would have appreciated if he'd asked me outright, "Why didn't you fix the bug?"

Asking questions might not help where trust between you and a person is low. They will probably react defensively to any questions, and you are unlikely to get an honest answer from them. If you can't put them at ease and convince them you genuinely care about their opinion, don't ask questions, because it may cause more harm than good. Instead, be direct and open, share your advice, and keep working on building rapport.

3.3 Encouraging Learning

Your team will need time to learn about Agile before they can adopt Agile practices. Encourage them to allow time for learning in their plans. For example, if the team wants to implement a new practice like Test-Driven Development, they'll need to allow time to learn how to do it before implementing it.

There's no need to drip-feed the team Agile ideas. Rather than relying on you as their sole source of knowledge about Agile, encourage them to take the initiative to learn about it for themselves.

Study Group

A study group (see *Fearless Change* (MR04)) is a regular informal meeting where a small group of people discuss an idea or chapter of a book. Five to ten people meeting weekly works well.

Work with the team to set these up to run at lunchtime, after work, or even during work time if the company supports such activities. People can bring their own lunch, or you may be able to persuade management to buy sandwiches or pizza. Each week the facilitator of the meeting rotates. Typically she presents a book chapter, and then the whole group discusses it. The meeting is small, so everyone can pitch into the discussion rather than listen to one person lecture.

This kind of meeting works well for several reasons. There is no teacher or expert present, which enables everyone to be an active participant and to draw their own conclusions. People learn more from reading and discussion, as compared to reading alone.

A study group is not just a way to get more information. It can provide support for people to try out the practices discussed. For example, after a study group session discusses pair programming or creates an automated deployment script, members of the study group may be inspired to try doing this themselves. Instead of reading about these ideas in isolation, they know they have support from their study group.

Creating Learning Opportunities

Agile practice is still evolving, so you and the team need to keep abreast of the current state of the art. There are many different ways to learn about Agile. Try to make it easy for people to access a variety of learning resources. For example, you can create a wiki page of useful links to books, articles, and podcasts.

Model the behavior yourself that you'd like to see in others. Let the team see that you spend time on your own learning, and talk to them about new things you've learned.

A powerful way to introduce new ideas is to arrange talks from people within the organization on their Agile experiences. This creates an opportunity for your colleagues to demonstrate what they've learned. It increases their kudos in the company and gives them an opportunity to practice public speaking. Giving a talk at work can even be the first stepping stone to speaking at an industry conference.

Tech Talks
by Liz

One company I worked at ran "tech talks," which started off being largely technically focused. Teams presented the work they had been doing at a technical level to the wider organization. Over time the topics of the talks broadened, and we had talks from the sales department about their concerns, talks from the CEO about his vision, talks about good GUI design, and so on.

You can generate interest by bringing in a expert to give a lecture. If you know that a well-known presenter will be visiting your city, then don't be afraid ask them. They may be interested in expanding their network and happy to come, especially if you offer to take them out for a beer and a meal afterward. You could also invite someone from your local Agile user group to come in and give a talk about how Agile works in their organization.

You can support the team's participation in study groups and lectures by being organized, booking meeting rooms, sending invites, inviting guest speakers, ordering lunch, and so on. Advertise these groups to attendees, and then readvertise them, especially on the day of the talk.

Going Outside the Organization to Learn

Conferences are also a great way to expose the team to new ideas. They provide an opportunity to meet people with the same problems, to share experiences, and to get support. For people who have been with the organization a long time, getting out to a conference can open their eyes to new ways of doing things.

Consider it part of your role to make people aware of how to find funding to attend conferences. When someone attends a conference, encourage them to share what they learned at the conference with the rest of the team. Make this request before they go so they are on the lookout for ideas to bring back to the team.

Your team can also find support and learn new ideas at a local user group. Rather than just letting them know about the next Agile group meeting, you can let them know that you'll be going and invite them to come with you.

3.4 Facilitating Meetings

Once the team is open to trying a change, don't throw everyone in the deep end and leave them floundering. When introducing a new practice to the team, show the team how it's done.

The first time the team tries a new Agile meeting, such as a retrospective or planning meeting, offer to *facilitate* the meeting to show them how it's done. During the meeting, explain the process you're following to the team so they can learn how to facilitate the meeting themselves. The next time around, sit down to plan the meeting with the person who will facilitate it, and then during the meeting, take a backseat. You can still jump in if the meeting gets off-track but otherwise leave your coach's feedback until the end.

Expose your thinking process to them by giving a running commentary. You might say, "I'm noticing that we've been in here for an hour, and it's getting quite stuffy. Let's take a break." Or "Darren, you're full of ideas today. But I notice Alison hasn't shared her thoughts on this story yet. Alison, do you have anything to add?"

Here are some tips to help make your meetings effective.

Choose a time: Establish a meeting time that works for the whole team, and give them plenty of notice about any preparation they need to do.

Set up the space: Consider what kind of space you want for the meeting. Avoid meeting rooms with very large tables because this spreads the team too far apart to see index cards on the table. You'll also need something to capture notes on, such as a flip chart or whiteboard.

Focus the meeting: Start the meeting by clearly stating the purpose of the meeting and giving a quick overview of the agenda. Remind the team of any working agreements or ground rules for meetings.

Keep it flowing: Stay on your toes during the meeting, and ensure the conversations in the meeting stay on topic and are productive. When you act as a "facilitator," your aim is to make the meeting easier for the people in it—like oil in an engine. You keep the meeting moving and focused on producing useful output. This is easier to do if you are not taking an active position in the discussion— step back to maintain a neutral position. If you need to offer an opinion, then explicitly step out of the facilitator role.

Encourage everyone to participate: Make sure everyone's opinion is heard. This means only one person talking at a time. When someone is making broad generalizations, it can help to ask for examples and ask clarifying questions to draw out the details.

Summarize key points: Before you write up any points on the whiteboard, check to see you have really understood the point by repeating what you heard.

Close the meeting: When you bring the meeting to a close, make sure that outputs are recorded appropriately. Taking digital photographs is a quick way to capture whiteboard sketches and meeting notes.

To improve next time, ask for feedback on your facilitation of the meeting. You can do this by asking everyone for suggestions at the end of the meeting or by asking someone to observe how you run the meeting and then discussing improvements with them after it finishes.

3.5 Hurdles

The following are some hurdles you may encounter.

Some People Don't Change

Some people like to be the first to try new things or to own the latest gadget. Others prefer to be the last, taking on change only when absolutely necessary. Don't get hung up on trying to convince laggards. They *prefer* to be the last to adopt a new way of working. They'll eventually change when Agile becomes the new status quo.

Bumping into Company Politics

When you introduce change, you are sometimes perceived as a threat to the existing balance of power. This will cause you to bump into company politics.

People who aren't very good at their jobs are likely to be exposed. Some people, like project managers or architects, may even believe that their job is under threat. Watch out for any misconceptions that need to be debunked.

A respected technical lead or manager may be the blocker to the team becoming more Agile. It won't help your cause if you're overly critical of him. Disagreeing with him in public can undermine him and cause him to lose face. Instead, spend time getting to know him so you understand his perspective. Then you can work on winning him over to your way of thinking by letting him know your plans so that you can gain his support.

You also need to be careful that you don't get too closely aligned with an authority figure like a tech lead or manager. If you have a senior sponsor, take special care not to support this person too much or reinforce their likes and dislikes. This person already has authority on their side; make it clear that you're not a spy from management and you're there to serve the team.

Conflicting Agendas

Sometimes it's hard to maintain your focus when others are looking to you for support. For instance, someone may come to you with complaints about not being allowed to stick things on the wall. You may agree that this is a problem but think it's not the right time to try to solve this.

Try to be neutral in public, and then explain in private that you are "picking your battles" to avoid getting a reputation for being negative. Explain the problems you are currently working to solve right now, and ask for their help.

Then you can work together on a plan for introducing their change or agree that it is a battle you won't be able to work on at the moment.

3.6 Checklist

- Share your passion for Agile, without being too fanatical. Talk about it, demonstrate it, and offer to help others with it. Encourage and inspire the team that Agile can and does work.

- Sell the problem to the team. Help them see why they need to change. What are the long-term implications of staying with the status quo? Also talk to the team members individually. How will they personally benefit from the change?

- When you meet resistance, try to understand where it's coming from. Is the problem with the idea or with the way you presented it? Are there good reasons to be concerned about the proposed idea? Are you listening properly to their concerns?

- Ask questions to engage the team in improving their Agile process. Try asking for help to enlist support, ask thinking questions to provoke reflection, and use Five Whys for root cause analysis.

- Encourage different ways to learn about Agile: leave books around the office, share blogs that you read, and point people to podcasts. Organize presentations and study groups that are open to other teams in the organization. Let people know about upcoming Agile events, and take people with you to the local Agile user group.

- Make new meetings easy for the team by facilitating them the first time around. Give them a running commentary so they can hear your thought process about running the meeting. The next time, help the team prepare for the meeting, and give them feedback afterward.

Chapter 4

Building an Agile Team

Working in a close Agile team is exciting. But cohesive teams don't just spring up in an instant; they take time to jell. When a team doesn't pull together, people get frustrated. The software they produce will reflect this.

You can help a team jell by establishing the conditions for teamwork to happen. Start by making time for them to get to know each other. Improve the workspace so the team has an environment that supports working together. Look for ways that you can help the team build a shared sense of where the project is headed.

4.1 Helping a Team Jell

An effective team seems to run like a well-oiled machine. Watch carefully, and you'll see they're not just following routines. When they hit problems, they adapt the way they work. When something needs doing, someone steps up to do it.

Social Glue

Teams take time to jell; it takes time to get to know everyone and to build trust. By working together, the team will start to understand one another's perspective and problems. Meetings, especially the daily standup and retrospectives, provide an opportunity to learn about each other.

Create opportunities for people to get to know each other better. You could try sharing personal histories (see the sidebar on page 49) or arrange a team outing, such as a meal or bowling. When the team

Liz Says...

Eat Lunch Together

Eat lunch with the team whenever you can. Listening to the team in an informal setting helps you understand them better.

You'll find teams often talk about the problems they're facing over lunch—in a way they wouldn't at a retrospective. For example, they might be truthful but rude about someone in a way that wouldn't be appropriate in a team meeting.

Dreamed-for process improvements are also discussed, again in a nonspecific, non-action-taking way that wouldn't be appropriate in a retrospective.

I got into the habit of taking a pen and some index cards to lunch, because they fit easily into my pocket. There's always something I want to remember or follow up on.

relaxes together, some of these stories come out in conversation. This helps create social glue that binds the team together.

Build Trust

Team collaboration requires trust. George Dinwiddie writes, "Trust builds on reasonable self-disclosure. You don't have to tell everything about yourself, but you can't be secretive, either."[1] You can lead the team in building trust by showing that it's safe to be open. Be transparent about your motives, and disclose information about your experience, your opinions, and your feelings—doing this invites openness from others. Admit when you make a mistake. Ask for help regularly.

But trust cannot take root when people don't feel safe. If there is a blame culture or people are criticized for mistakes, they won't feel safe. Team members need to be comfortable to admit when they need help. When the team feels safe, they will be happy to share advice and help each other.

---

1. http://blog.gdinwiddie.com/2008/12/03/aye-2008-the-magic-chemistry-of-teams/

Sharing Personal Histories

In *Overcoming the Five Dysfunctions of a Team* (Len05) Patrick Lencioni recommends you help a team get comfortable with openness by taking the time to share personal histories.

He suggests running an exercise where each member of the team tells a story about a challenge they faced in the past. This could be a story from their childhood, school, or first job, starting with some basic information such as where they're from and how many brothers and sisters they had.

As each team member tells their story, they have an opportunity to practice being open with their teammates. As the people on the team hear the stories, they get a better insight into each storyteller, and knowing something personal about them helps create empathy.

Lencioni stresses the purpose of the exercise should be made clear to the team from the outset. You also need to take care that everyone understands they are not being asked to reveal anything they feel uncomfortable sharing.

If people feel really unsafe—for example, if they are scared that they will lose their jobs—you won't be able to do any Agile coaching. In this case, you will need to support the team in any way you can until the situation resolves itself.

Trust Requires Safety
by Rachel

I worked with one company where Brian, the IT manager, was concerned about the lack of openness in his teams. The teams went through the motions of daily standup meetings, but there seemed to be a lack of trust. People kept quiet when they were stuck and didn't ask for help.

Brian held a scrum of scrums meeting in his office every day at noon, which was attended by all the team leads and project managers. I attended this meeting as an observer.

Brian ran the meeting. I noticed that he took great glee in shaking a pot to collect fines from anyone who was late. As he went around the circle, asking each person for their report, he fired off remarks that put them off their guard. He seemed to know how to take the wind out of their sails every time, chiding them for past mistakes and reminding them of the consequences of delivering late. Everyone knew he did not suffer fools gladly and that staff had been laid off recently.

It seemed that Brian's communication style had a lot to do with the lack of trust in his department. He needed to learn when it was appropriate to give feedback and when to keep quiet and listen.

Bridge the Gap

Building trust between different roles, such as developers, testers, analysts, and technical authors, also takes time. You can help the team bridge the gap between different disciplines by suggesting they take on another role for a short period. For example, a developer could take on a testing role for a week. If they do not have the required skills to do the other role, they can pair with someone and contribute as much as they can. Walking "a mile in their moccasins" will help them get a better understanding of the work.

People may not understand what their teammates do and assume their own role is harder. But without mutual respect, the team will not flourish. You can demonstrate respect for everyone on the team by asking for opinions and help and by taking their concerns and problems seriously. Others will notice this and imitate you.

If a person on the team seems unhappy with another team member, invite them for coffee, and discuss it. What assumptions has she made that has caused her to think that way about her team member? What alternative explanations are there?

4.2 Creating a Team Space

A team needs a shared workspace to keep communication flowing. The ideal is for the whole team—and no one else—to sit together in the same room. A "break-out area" near the team, where they can get a cup of coffee and chat, allows the team to relax and build friendships. A meeting room nearby is useful for privacy or for having discussions without interrupting the team.

However, some people may be reluctant to move desks or sit together because an open plan workspace can feel exposed and impersonal. Encourage the team to design their own workspace and customize it to suit them. It's amazing how a few plants, books, and pictures can make a space feel safer to work in.

> ### Type Assessments
>
> To help the team get a better sense of their individual strengths and weaknesses, the team might like to try type profiling. Suggest to the team that they take a Myers-Briggs Type Indicator (MBTI)* or Belbin Self-Perception Inventory† assessment.
>
> If they agree, then each person on the team takes the assessment individually and shares the results with the team. These tests are not an assessment of performance or ability, but they rather explore interaction preferences and behavioral tendencies of team members. Sharing the results can help the team better understand each other's behavior.
>
> *. http://www.myersbriggs.org/
> †. http://www.belbin.com/

Sometimes when companies adopt Agile, it takes them a long time to realize that this is not just about how developers work; it requires change across the whole organization. Consequently, you may find a lot of resistance to the idea that a tester should sit next to a developer, who is in turn sitting next to a product manager. Campaign tirelessly for this, because it is hard to build an Agile team when people are segregated.

Once everyone is sitting together, they can get started on building an *informative workspace*, where useful information is displayed to help people structure their time and make good decisions. We'll guide you through setting this up in Chapter 8, *Keeping It Visible*, on page 107.

It's not just the physical workspace that you need to pay attention to. The virtual environment needs to support collaboration too. Arrange a session with the team to work out where they want to keep electronic information. Encourage them to set up a wiki or shared repository for documents rather than relying on shared network drives. They also need to be clear about the consistent setup of development and testing environments.

4.3 Balancing Roles

The relationship between customers and developers is crucial because they need to work together to create the best product. Everyone needs to feel like they are part of the same team, working toward the same goal. Make role responsibilities clear to the whole team.

The customer[2] is the person who owns the business case and prioritizes what the software should do. The development team takes responsibility for deciding how to build it and communicating to the customer how long that takes. The customer can set the dates that they require software to be delivered, but they don't nail down scope—that's worked out with the team.

Often the customer is a product manager who works with multiple users and stakeholders to decide what the software should do. On large developments, the customer role can be too big for one person, so a customer team is formed. This team needs to contain all the necessary expertise to work out the user stories and prioritize them. Your customer team might include business analysts, user representatives, and interaction designers—the exact mix depends on the project and the organization.

Sometimes the best solution is a "near-customer," who helps work out the details of the requirements with the team, and a "far-customer," who makes the decisions about business priorities. The near-customer could be played by a business analyst who sits with the team, while the far-customer is a product manager who sits closer to the business operations and marketing teams.

If the roles get out of balance, one side or the other will be overworked. If the customer is overworked, then developers don't get enough of their time and are left to guess at what they want. If there are not enough developers or they are working slower than expected, the business will be disappointed with their output. You can help as a coach by making the side effects of the imbalance more visible so management can consider addressing this problem.

4.4 Energizing the Team

Great teams are self-motivated. Sometimes, though, we find a team gets stuck—they're not sure how to get started. There may be big opportunities, but they can't see the wood for the trees and are overwhelmed. The following are some ideas about how to energize the team and help them find their own motivation.

---

2. This generic term is roughly equivalent to the product owner role in Scrum.

Not Too Easy, Not Too Hard

The secret to great teams is they need reachable but challenging goals. Everyone needs to be sufficiently challenged, neither bored nor anxious. This is the optimum work zone where people enjoy it the most.

If work is too easy, developers will get bored and demotivated. They won't be proud of achieving something easy. If there is a lot of easy work to be done, encourage them to find ways to automate it.

Sometimes the work seems to be impossible and far beyond their comfort zone. This can paralyze the team. They need to break down the work into manageable chunks. Can they find something that they can get started on? If more investigation is needed before they can figure out what to do next, encourage them to experiment and try their ideas.

Foster a culture where it's OK to experiment to learn more about a problem that the team is trying to solve. As Thomas Edison famously said, "I have not failed. I've just found 10,000 ways that won't work." If the team doesn't have enough information to choose between two or three ways of doing things, they could try them all out. After each experiment, the team will know more. Although developing more than one solution may feel like a waste of time, it can be a quick way to learn and a cheap way to mitigate the risk of making the wrong decision.

Find a Compelling Goal

Knowing they are producing a useful product should help the team engage. Although as a coach you can't set the product direction, you can help the team understand the big picture and the team mission. If you can, arrange for the team to meet end users. User needs will be more vivid to the team and give them ideas of how they can help make a better product.

You can also help paint the picture of the opportunities within the project and how it might connect with their personal goals. Agile teams plan and design their own work. Be clear how much latitude and autonomy they have over how the software is designed, built, and tested. Once they understand that they don't need to wait for permission, it can free them to make a start.

Time for Innovation

We've met developers on Agile projects who were burned out by working on a continuous stream of user stories.

If they don't get time to explore new technology or experiment with innovative product ideas, teams become demotivated. Make time in iteration plans for them to explore new ideas. This can do wonders for motivation—and for the product.

When team members get time to experiment with new ideas, clean up things that bug them, or learn something new, then they become happier at work. This improves the energy of the team and rubs off on project tasks too. Help the team find their own mini-projects within each project by listening to them and encouraging them to follow up on their ideas.

Gold Cards
by Rachel

I worked with a team who implemented *gold cards* (see "Innovation and Sustainability with Gold Cards" presented at XP Universe 2001 Conference [HMMP]) to address this problem. Developers got the opportunity to play a gold card and work on a topic of their choice for the day rather than a task on the team board. Each developer on the team got two gold cards per month, and they would announce their decision to play their gold card at the daily standup.

We spent our gold card time on all sorts of things: trying new tools, working on new product ideas, and learning something new. At the end of every iteration, we showed the rest of the team what we'd done.

In this team, the gold card work led to changes in both the product we were working on and our supporting infrastructure—it was definitely time well spent.

Gold cards provide a way for the team to present new product ideas to their customer to make it a product they're proud of. It is also a way for them to get to do challenging work. We've found it can be effective for all the developers to take their gold cards on the same day every week. This enables developers to work on their ideas together and makes them feel it is OK to not work on the project for a day. Take a look at the full paper for how to sell gold cards to management; one angle is that gold cards create a basis for individual performance reviews without detracting from team collaboration.

Celebrate Success

Find ways to celebrate the success of every release. Having a team lunch or drinks celebrates success and increases team bonding. Help the team find ways to demonstrate their success to other teams and the wider organization. They could invite people to their iteration demo, show the product at a company meeting, or send out an announcement.

The team will get a boost when other people notice they are successful and appreciate them. A word of thanks from management or customers is important; consider prompting them to do this. Getting feedback from users, especially if their lives have now been improved, is motivating. One company Liz worked with displayed emails, from happy customers and unhappy customers, prominently on the wall by the coffee machine.

How Are We Doing?
by Rachel

I once worked with a team that was on what they perceived as a dull legacy project. It really boosted their morale after the initial release to hear how much money it generated for the company in the week after it went live. Their project had really been noticed and was making a difference.

Don't Demotivate

People start off motivated. If nothing demotivates them, there's a good chance they'll stay motivated! What makes people happy and motivated at work is what they do. What makes people unhappy and demotivated at work is the situation in which they do it. Situational problems include stress and the company culture.

In *The Motivation to Work* [Her93] Frederick Herzberg explains *hygiene factors*. These are factors that demotivate people if they are not present, even though these factors aren't motivators when they are present. For instance, fast computers, decent coffee, and fair pay won't be noticed if they are there, but their absence can demotivate employees. Although some of these hygiene factors may be things outside your influence as a coach, it's worth talking to the team about what annoys them. You may find some things that can easily be fixed, such as improving their work environment.

Beware of Incentives

Be careful about using "incentives" to motivate people. As Alfie Kohn explains in *Punished by Rewards* [Koh93], incentive schemes aimed at encouraging individual productivity can damage collaboration within the team because helping out a teammate doesn't make sense if developers are competing for a bonus.

If the team is being offered a bonus for doing their job, they will often do only what is needed to achieve the reward, no more and no less. If management must have a bonus scheme, then ask them to base it on achieving a team or company goal—not an individual one. The team will work better when they're motivated by the satisfaction of doing a good job and producing a great product.

4.5 Hurdles

The following are some hurdles you may encounter.

Teams Aren't Cross-Functional

Some companies organize teams by discipline, such as analysts, designers, testers, software engineers, and so on, with separate reporting lines. This is a serious blocker to becoming Agile because a fundamental Agile principle is cross-functional teams with different disciplines working together to build the best software. For Agile to work effectively, everyone should be empowered to work on the project at the same time to avoid hand-offs between disciplines that cause delays.

If you're coaching a software development team in this situation, campaign to get additional team members from other disciplines, such as testers and analysts. Work on building good relationships between the development team and people with other disciplines allocated part-time to the project. Invite these virtual team members to all the Agile meetings, and include them on emails. Organize a social meal or drink to help everyone feel like a team.

No On-Site Customer

Sometimes the development team is in one location and the customer is working from another office. They may even be in a different time zone, particularly if they need to be close to the end users who are in a different country. If not handled well, working with a remote customer can cause communication problems and resentment.

Building a good relationship with the remote customer is vital in this situation. Encourage this customer to visit and meet with everyone in the team face-to-face so that they know each other. The first planning meeting is often a good opportunity to do this. Afterward, you can encourage regular conversations by phone and more informal channels such as instant messaging or a shared chat room.

Remember the proverb "out of sight, out of mind." Humans are wired to respond to seeing faces. Try to get webcams that the team can use to see people in other offices, at their desktop computers and for use in teleconferences. Surprisingly, even having static photos of the people not in the room can make a difference.

Team Is Too Big

If you are working with a team with more than ten members, this is likely to have an effect on communication and responsibility within the team. Any meeting with a large number of people takes longer and makes it harder for everyone to stay engaged. Each person will feel less committed to the team goal because their individual responsibility to the team is less. Work with the team to find a way to break the project into subteams—ideally feature teams. *Scaling Lean and Agile Development* [LV09] has some advice on how feature teams work.

Team Is a Resource Pool

Agile doesn't work well when a pool of people working on several projects try to apply Agile as if they were a single team. Agile assumes one project at a time. When the team is working on multiple projects, there's no big compelling goal. You'll notice that priorities on the different projects change, and this causes interruptions that must be juggled within the team. We recommend that you don't apply Agile in this situation.

Team Members Ostracize Someone on Their Team

You may notice that the team avoids working with one person on the team. Is this problem because of lack of trust? Or is it a practical problem? Maybe that person doesn't shower in the morning?

Try talking to the team (when the person being avoided is not around) to see whether they have an explanation. Also talk to the ostracized person. Are they aware of the situation? Involve HR if you're worried that they're distracted from work because of illness, stress, or depression.

Team Becomes Complacent

Teams often become insular when there is a lack of exposure to other teams and business goals. If you become concerned about the team being too complacent, it may be worth trying to increase the visibility of the team's work to senior stakeholders and increase the feedback to the team about business value generated by their work.

4.6 Checklist

- Create opportunities for the team to get to know each other, which helps the team jell. Regularly spend informal time together, such as lunch or drinks.

- Create a shared workspace to help the team work together well. Try to get the whole team sitting together.

- Make role responsibilities clear. Get the customer the support they need to work within the team.

- Ensure the team has a reachable but challenging goal. Make sure the work is neither too easy nor too hard.

- Arrange food or drink to celebrate a release. Ask customers and management to thank the team.

Part II

Planning as a Team

Chapter 5

Daily Standup

You've already taken part in many daily standup meetings, so you may be surprised to find a whole chapter about them. They seem easy to implement. All you need to do is bring the team together to stand in a circle at the same time every day and have them answer three simple questions:

- What did I do yesterday?
- What will I do today?
- What's in my way?

These three questions are a good start, but they're more like training wheels for the team. As a coach, you can take the team beyond this format and help them customize the meeting to suit their needs. You want the team to adopt the daily standup as their own meeting; it's where they decide who's working on what, and it encourages them to self-organize. Once the team learns how to drive the daily standup, a coach takes a backseat.

You'll find the daily standup reveals how well the team members are working together. Watch out for daily standups that are a shallow status update to a manager, where the people on the team don't really listen to each other. Notice if the meeting drags on, if it wastes the team's valuable time by going into too much detail, or if it lasts half an hour or more. When it's quick, high-energy, and self-managed, then the team is on the right track. Another good sign is when the team runs a daily standup even when you're not around.

There's an art to getting the right balance of information sharing in the daily standup. Let's look at what you can do to get these meetings off to a good start with the team.

Rachel Says...

Follow Your Own Advice

Be a role model by following your own advice. At the daily standup, make sure that you're ready for the meeting on time. When it's running, stand firmly on two feet rather than slumping against a desk or wall. If you don't take the meeting seriously, why should anyone else?

Modeling the behavior that you expect from the team is an important coaching technique. Adopt the behavior you'd like to see from the team, and it rubs off on them.

5.1 Standing Up

At first, the team may be uncomfortable about having a meeting where they stand rather than sit in a meeting room, especially if they're working in a more traditional organization. People can be self-conscious about standing up where others can see them—it can seem odd, even eccentric! Make sure the team knows that there is a good reason for standing; the meeting takes less time when everyone is on their feet. This is likely to win them over—most people want to spend less of their work time in meetings.

We find reservations disappear after the team has experienced what a daily standup is like. If they're reluctant, ask the them to try standing up for the meeting for a couple of weeks. Frame this as an experiment with the opportunity to review how they feel about it in their next retrospective. If they also want to try the daily standup as a sitdown meeting, track the time the meeting takes so you have some evidence on whether standing up really does keep it short.

The daily standup works best when it's held in the team workspace around the team board. The team needs enough room to stand in a semicircle so that they can see each other and the board. Encourage them to move the furniture to make a good space for the daily standup. If there's just not enough room in their workspace, look for space nearby. Where meeting rooms are scarce, be creative—we've worked with teams who used a spacious stair landing for their daily standups.

If the team has to run the daily standup away from their team workspace, it's more disruptive because of the shuffle time to get there and get back. It can also be a problem because they need to talk about tasks on their team board. Some teams solve this by taking over a meeting room and maintaining their team board and charts on the walls of this "scrum room."

We're not fans of this approach because they can't see the tasks during the rest of the day—their team board ceases to be an *information radiator*. They'll be better off creating a portable team board that can be taken along to the daily standup and then brought back to the team space. We'll talk more about how you can help them do this in Chapter 8, *Keeping It Visible*, on page 107.

5.2 For the Team by the Team

It's essential to get the message across to the team that their daily standup is for *them* to synchronize *their* work. It is *not* held for a project manager or team lead to gather progress from the team or give feedback on their work. Encourage the team to direct their answers toward other team members.

Keep conversation focused on the work in the plan; if someone is just back from vacation, this is not the time to discuss their trip. The team doesn't need to mention work done on other projects unless it is seriously hampering their ability to complete their work. Be polite, but if this happens, remind the team of the purpose of the daily standup and get it moving again.

When the daily standup is new to the team, you can nudge the conversation along. If a person hesitates, prompt them with one of the three questions. When people have been working in a pair, it's fine for only one of the pair to summarize what they did. Once the team gets used to the daily standup, you'll find they naturally move away from the three-question format and include additional questions. The team can add reminders about these new questions to their team board.

Nudge conversation along.

Standup Chekov

WHAT WE DID YESTERDAY
ANY NEW CARDS?
SALES MEETINGS?
WHO IS EXPOSED TODAY?
MARK TIME SPENT
PICK CARDS AND PARTNERS

Standup Chekov
by Rachel

I worked in an XP team where we posted a checklist on our team board to remind us what to cover at our daily standup. We called this list the "Standup Chekov," and we posted a sign on our team board with a picture of Pavel Chekhov, a character from the original *Star Trek* TV series to remind us to check off our Chekov questions.

You'll notice we moved on from the three-question format. We had some other items we wanted to cover, mostly related to customer support. For instance, every day we took turns to make sure that some developers were designated "Exposed," which meant interruptible for sales and customer support issues. At the time, we were experimenting with tracking time spent per story so we could improve our estimates. But the most crucial question that we used this meeting for was who would be pair programming together.

Our team later added some other Chekovs to remind them about other things, such as getting a story done.

Establishing a Team Focus

Watch out—if you're always asking the questions in the daily standup, you may find that team members direct their replies to you, as if the meeting is for your benefit, not theirs. Try to deflect this by not meeting their gaze and looking around the circle at the team.

If you notice that team members continue to treat the meeting as a report to you, come right out and say, "Please, can you direct your replies to the whole team? The daily standup is for you all to work out what you need to do today, not me." You can also try not attending the daily standup at all, leaving the team to run it without you.

Avoid giving praise, saying "Great!" or even "Thank you" after someone lets the team know what they completed. This reinforces the impression that the daily standup is about pleasing you rather than synchronizing the team's activities. When you give a single word of praise, it can leave the recipient puzzled. Did you mean that they did a good job? What aspect of their work was great? You'll also leave the team wondering why some people get praise while others don't.

Team Controls the Flow

Encourage the team to take control of their daily standup. To make this explicit, introduce a speaking token that is passed from one person to the next. The token can be any object (such as a ball or marker pen), which each speaker holds when they have something to say. Each team member takes the token when they are speaking and decides who to pass it onto next. There's no single point of control. This helps keep the meeting flowing, and the person who holds the token becomes more aware of the rest of the team waiting.

If someone can't attend the daily standup and is phoning into the meeting, a mobile phone handset works well as the speaking token. It enables the person at the other end to hear, while keeping everyone focused on talking to the team rather than talking to the phone. The team might decide to stop using a speaking token later when they're used to how the daily standup flows.

Here's a sample of a typical round of conversation that you might hear at a daily standup.

Tuesday Morning

Damian starts the daily standup. "OK, I'll get the ball rolling. Yesterday, I worked on processing the new data feed. I checked it in, but I noticed it seems to stall partway through—it's not bringing in all of the book blurbs. So today, I'll be trying to work out what's happening with that before I pick up another task. No other blockers for me. Catch!" he says tossing Larry the tennis ball that the team uses as a speaking token.

Larry, who's looking rather sleepy today, jumps with surprise and just manages to catch the ball. "Well, I've been working on setting up test data. I've created some XML files by sampling the data feed, and I checked them into SVN last night. Today, I want to start testing the book carousel, if it's ready?" he says holding the ball out to Rebecca.

Rebecca takes the token. "Well," hesitates Rebecca, "it's not quite finished, but it would be good if you could take a quick look at what I've got so far."

"OK," Larry adds, "let's do that this morning. While you're getting ready, I'll make a start on the test scripts for the recommendations engine."

Rebecca continues with her update. "So yesterday. . . I worked on the carousel. It's going pretty well, but I haven't done any browser testing yet, so I expect Larry is going to find some problems. I'll probably be working on that for most of the day. Nothing is in my way. Joe?" asks Rebecca holding out the token.

Joe takes the token. "I got in early today and finished off ISBN search this morning, so that's ready for testing too. I won't be starting any new tasks just yet because Amanda has asked me to go to a teleconference with the Singapore team this morning."

"So, no issues you need me to follow up on with ops today?" asks Raj.

"Sorry to disappoint you, Raj!" grins Joe, and the team breaks up to get started with their tasks.

Notice the team in the story talks about the progress on the tasks rather than giving exhaustive accounts of what they did yesterday. Also, they're not trying to solve every problem that comes up. If Joe has some ideas about solving the problem that Damian has run into, they can chat about that after the meeting.

Only the people who actually worked on the tasks on the team board answered the questions. Raj is the project manager; he's there to follow up on any issues that come up rather than work on the tasks in the plan. Amanda is the product manager and acts as the customer for the team; she wasn't able to attend the daily standup, so she'll have to catch up with progress later in the day by asking someone who was there.

Who Takes Part

The whole team comes to daily standup: developers, testers, designers, customers, Agile coach, and so on. We have seen Agile teams tell customers (and other stakeholders) that they must stay silent because they are "chickens." Discourage this; it's disrespectful and can cause unnecessary upset. The team needs to build bridges with their stakeholders, not burn them.

The focus of the daily standup is the work in the current plan; the customer plays a part in this so she can let the team know what she's working on in the same way as anyone else on the team. The daily standup may also be the ideal time to pass information on to the team about upcoming work; such updates can be covered at the end of the meeting.

Watch out for conversations at daily standups that can't be followed by the whole team. If you close down a discussion during the daily standup because it's not relevant to everyone, remind them to get it going again straight after the daily standup with a smaller group.

Two-Part Daily Standup
by Rachel

I worked with one team that decided they would have a two-part daily standup. The first part was a catch-up for the development team about who worked on what and any issues. This was pretty dull for the customer team to listen to, because the conversation was full of references to technical jargon. We didn't exclude the customer team; they could see when the meeting started because we were standing up, and they were welcome to join us. In the second part, the development team would call the customer team over to let them know who would be working on the user stories and arrange any follow-up meetings to discuss details of the story tests.

This solution worked pretty well for the team. Now the team could have all the conversations they needed to start the day without wasting their customer's time.

5.3 Handling Issues

When someone on the team mentions an issue that's getting in their way, it's often best to leave the discussion of how to solve it until the end of the daily standup. The team won't have the full picture until everyone has spoken, and each issue may not require the whole team to solve it. Try to separate conversations out in the daily standup— invite the team to share progress before discussing how to resolve any issues. Quick clarifying questions are OK, but encourage the team to move on once they understand the problem.

There's no point asking about what got in the way if issues aren't followed up. Avoid saying "Let's take that offline" every time the conversation meanders or someone raises an issue, because this is ambiguous. Rather than scribbling notes about issues in your notebook, write each item that requires follow-up on a whiteboard that everyone can see to create a *parking lot* for issues. At the end of the meeting, revisit the parking lot to prioritize the items and work out who needs to be

Liz Says...

Forget the Formula

The Scrum method presents strict rules about who speaks and what should be said at the daily standup. It places great emphasis on starting on time.

Rules for running daily standup meetings are to help teams get started with them. There's no magic in this formula. These rules should not be a straightjacket imposed on the team forevermore. Sticking strictly to this formula makes the daily standup feel like it's "being done by numbers," which stifles self-organization within the team.

My advice is don't let these meetings lose sight of their purpose. I am happier to hear animated discussions and see everyone engaged than see the Scrum formula being executed like clockwork.

involved in any follow-up. Any issues addressed in the daily standup can be wiped off, if they've been resolved. There's no need to log them, although if they are getting a lot of interruptions from outside, the team may decide to track time wasted on handling them.

The daily standup should not be a substitute for other meetings. If it throws up the need for a longer discussion with the whole team, suggest the team arranges a meeting to cover it rather than tacking on a conversation to the end of their daily standup.

As well as the issues mentioned by the team, you can check whether they have any dependencies on items being delivered by people outside the team. Some typical examples are software interfaces, editorial copy, design assets, database changes, and so on. The team will probably evolve the layout of their team board over time so that it incorporates reminders to follow such things up.

5.4 Setting the Time

Most teams prefer to have the daily standup at the start of the working day to discuss who's working on what before getting immersed in their work. However, in many companies, people don't arrive at work at the same time, so they need to find a time for the meeting that works for everyone.

As a coach, you shouldn't pick the meeting time. Instead, ask the team when they want the daily standup. This won't make the decision any easier, but it builds team commitment to the time and promotes a culture of the team solving their own problems.

Make it a team decision.

Sometimes getting the whole team to the standup every day is a challenge. For example, some people may work from home, be in other meetings, or not work full-time on the project. Daily standups are even more of a challenge when the team is distributed between different offices and time zones. Remember what you're trying to achieve— good communication and everyone knowing what they need to work on. Encourage the team to experiment with different approaches until they find a good compromise.

Teleconference calls or alternating the time of the daily standup may work. Some people may need to be excused from the meeting and kept up-to-date in a different way. Perhaps colocated team members can have a face-to-face daily standup followed by a conference call with remote team members. For different time zones, that conversation might even be at the other end of the day.

Night People vs. Morning People
by Rachel

One company that I worked with offered very flexible working hours as a perk for all employees. Some team members didn't arrive in the office until after lunch and then worked late into the evening, while others came in early and finished work in the afternoon. This team chose an afternoon time for their daily standup, which helped them synchronize their work.

The downside was that the morning people had to start work without knowing where the rest of the team had got up to until the daily standup meeting after lunch. Teams split over time zones have the same issue and often run both morning and afternoon standup meetings. I suggested to the team that they try this. Now the morning people could sync up with each other before the night people came in.

5.5 When to Coach

If you're not directing the conversation and keeping the daily standup running to time, then where do you add value as a coach? Our view is that a coach acts as the conscience of the team—a bit like Jiminy Cricket in the children's film *Pinocchio*. For instance, you can gently remind the team about what they planned to do if they're straying from it. There's a real art to this; you don't want to come across as nagging, so try not to do this preemptively—you don't want to be the person always saying "Don't forget this" or "Don't forget that." Wait until they're actually drifting; then make an observation that what you see them doing is different than what they planned. Ask them whether it's really a problem and, if so, how they're planning to handle it.

The members of the team spend their days focused on implementing user stories, and they often don't notice how quickly time is passing. You can help by reminding the team about how many days before the next demo or release and asking them to check that the team board reflects what they're working on now.

It's not just the passing of time that you may need to remind the team about. They're following an iterative cycle. They need to take time, during each iteration, to work with their customer to get user stories ready for the next planning session. They also need to follow up on actions from their retrospective and get these done by the end of the iteration.

Sometimes the team doesn't raise problems because they have gotten used to them or think they are unsolvable. As a coach, keep an inquiring mind, and be on the lookout for opportunities for improvement. The daily standup often reveals areas where team members need coaching support. Read the team by listening to what is and isn't being said and noticing any odd body language:

- Is everyone engaged, motivated, and excited?

- Are they making progress and working on high-priority tasks?

- Are they working together and helping each other?

- Are they able to concentrate and do their job without interruptions?

Unless you are seriously concerned that the team has lost focus on the current plan, follow up on these observations after the meeting, or defer discussion until the next retrospective.

5.6 Hurdles

The following are some hurdles you may encounter.

People Arriving Late for the Meeting

Don't repeat information as latecomers arrive. This is disrespectful to everyone else and sends the message that it is OK to be late.

We've worked with teams who ask latecomers to pay a fine if they miss the start of the daily standup. This might work for the team, but be aware that some people may be happy to pay (and even feel good about being late if the pot of money is to be given to charity or a contribution to a team night out).

If a team member is consistently late, then talk to him about it. Try to understand what the problem is. Maybe his alarm clock is broken, or perhaps he's lost his interest in the work (see suggestions for unblocking motivation in Section 4.4, *Energizing the Team*, on page 52). Whatever the cause, something needs to change for him to participate in team meetings.

Help him become aware of his behavior, because this can be enough to trigger a change. Does he realize that arriving late is bothering his teammates? Explain the impact of his late arrival on others.

Big Visible Chart
by Rachel

I worked with a team where a senior developer, Vicky, was often late for the daily standup meeting. Vicky didn't realize how often she was coming in late—in her mind she was late only once or twice a month. Her behavior was starting to have a knock-on effect on the junior developers; if it was OK for Vicky to be late, then they could be too.

The team discussed this at their retrospective and proposed keeping a sign-up chart on their team board; every time a person was late for the daily standup, they would add their name to this list. Vicky didn't feel uncomfortable about this because she still didn't believe she was late that often. The chart provided a feedback mechanism for the team that helped them become aware of how often they were actually arriving late. After Vicky had put her name up a couple of times, she started to make extra efforts to arrive on time. The other team members followed suit, and by the second week, everyone was in the office in plenty of time for daily standup.

So, the chart designed to measure the problem actually helped reduce the problem. This is an example of how a team decision to track information visibly influences behavior.

Meeting Takes Too Long

If the daily standup regularly takes more than fifteen minutes, look for ways to speed it up. In this case, we do recommend sticking to the formula questions, with each team member giving their replies in turn and leaving discussions until the end.

Remind the team there's no need for them to list every single thing they did yesterday; cover only what's relevant for their teammates to get the big picture. Focus on what's relevant to the tasks being worked on today and what needs to happen to deliver the stories by the due date.

If you are working with a large team (more than ten members), you can speed up the daily standup by asking for an update on each user story rather than from each person. Although this may make the daily standup more bearable, it does not solve the underlying problem that it's difficult to create a sense of shared ownership with a large team.

In a daily standup meeting of this size, you'll probably notice that some team members aren't listening to other team members. The amount of work in progress has become too much for them to keep up with all the details. Some stories don't seem relevant to them. When people start caring only about their own tasks, teamwork starts to breaks down.

A better solution for large teams is to break into subteams that plan their work separately and have smaller daily standups. Then the sub-teams coordinate their work via a new meeting called a *scrum of scrums*.

Daily Standup Is Hijacked

The daily standup can also be taken over by someone who has noticed that this is a good time to nab the team for other discussions. This person is not necessarily disrupting the daily standup on purpose; this usually happens because they don't understand how the Agile life cycle works. Handle this by talking to the hijacker afterward rather than challenging them in the meeting.

Sometimes this person is from outside the team and comes to the daily standup because he wants the team to help him out with a piece of work, such as a support request or creating a demo for a sales meeting.

Explain that they're welcome to come along to the daily standup, but its focus has to be on the stories in the current plan. Recommend they talk with the customer about their requests, so these can be considered in the next planning meeting.

Another hijacker can be a manager or team lead.

Daily Standup Takeover
by Rachel

Ray was introducing Agile to his team. He set up a team room where the team held the daily standup meeting and kept their iteration plan on the wall. Every morning he led the way to the team room and pulled up a bean bag waiting for the rest of the team to join him. As they trooped in, they also pulled up bean bags and slumped down ready for Ray to start proceedings.

Ray ran the daily standup in two halves. The first half gave him a chance to gather team progress; the second half was dedicated to working through the issues and allocating work for the day. The daily standup usually took half an hour, but this was really a series of conversations between Ray and individual team members.

It wasn't a good use of their time, and it definitely wasn't encouraging the team to take ownership and self-organize. From their perspective, Ray could have achieved the same effect by going around to the individual team members while they were sitting at their desks. At least that way, they could get on with some work while he was talking to someone else.

I talked with Ray about the purpose of the daily standup, but he didn't seem to think that the way he ran it was a problem. So, I tried another angle; I asked him to come along to observe another team run their daily standup. This opened his eyes to the possibility that he could encourage his own team to report to each other and decide their own tasks.

You might be surprised, but it can be even worse than in the previous story. Another sitdown daily standup was run by a program manager passing around a spreadsheet to her team. The team filled the spreadsheet in without talking at all.

Don't criticize a person who doesn't know how to run the daily standup. You'll find that the remedy lies in education about how Agile works. Can you arrange for the person running the daily standup to get some Agile training? Try taking them along to see how another team in your organization runs their daily standup. You could also suggest that you run the next daily standup to give them an example of how to do it.

When they try applying what they learned, be an observer, and then follow up by giving them feedback after the daily standup.

The Team Isn't Working on the Planned Tasks

Often the tasks for a user story change when the team starts working on them, because they've learned more about what actually needs to be done. Encourage the team to add cards to represent new tasks on the team board so it's clear what the current plan is. Also remind them to remove any tasks that they're not planning to do anymore. Now it's easier to match up what is said in the daily standup with the tasks on the team board.

Notice if members of the team are working on another project instead of the stories in this project; this may lead to them not delivering the stories in the current plan. If there's a risk of this, then encourage the team to flag it up to their customer.

Unplanned work often also comes up when the team is supporting a live product, as well as developing new features for that product. This situation is very common for Agile teams who deploy software early on in the project. We recommend working with the customer to establish a budget for support (in developer days) and tracking how much time is being spent on support against that. Try using different-colored cards, on the team board, for support tasks so that it's very visible if they're being prioritized over new product development.

Daily Standup Isn't Wanted

Daily standups can seem scary because everyone is exposed. When the team is not getting tasks done, it becomes visible at the standup. If a person on the team objects to taking part in daily standups, check how much progress they're making on their tasks, just in case they're stuck and trying to hide out.

However, if the whole team objects to the daily standups, you have a more serious problem on your hands. It is possible that they're struggling to work as a team or that the meetings are being badly run. We suggest you discuss their concerns in the retrospective.

Not Everyone Can Stand

You may have a member of the team who has health reasons for not standing during a daily standup, such as when someone has a bad back or is pregnant. Look for a way to accommodate their needs in a way that helps them feel integrated in the team. If the rest of the team is standing, then make sure that this person is part of the team circle *without* people standing in front or behind them. You don't want this person to end up in the center of the circle or outside it. Consider running the daily standup as a sitdown meeting so everyone is on the same level, but be aware that if you sit down, it's likely to take longer.

5.7 Checklist

- Find a space that the team can run their daily standup around their team board. If they don't have room in their workspace, then use a portable team board.

- Make the time that the daily standup runs a team decision. You can run it more than once a day, if not everyone works the same hours.

- Encourage the team to keep their replies short and sweet. The three-question formula can help the team get started, but don't let this become a straightjacket for daily standup conversation.

- Keep the daily standup flowing; a speaking token puts this in control of the team.

- Ask the customer along to the daily standup to give her progress and updates.

- Gather issues that come up on a whiteboard where everyone can see them. Prioritize it with the team, and follow up afterward.

- Review the effectiveness of the daily standup in the retrospective, and experiment with the format.

Chapter 6

Understanding What to Build

If the team members want to deliver valuable software, they need to go the extra mile to understand both user and business benefits, and user stories help them do that. User stories underpin all the work an Agile team does—they're the basis of plans, development, and testing.

We find teams often struggle making the shift to user stories because they treat user stories as requirements documents, passively accepting them without asking questions. They're missing a trick; the whole point of user stories is to ask questions to better understand what users need and to find ways of breaking requirements down.

In this chapter, we'll explore how to introduce user stories to the team and avoid common pitfalls.

6.1 Life Cycle of a User Story

Let's walk through the life cycle of a user story by comparing it to the life cycle of a butterfly.

A user story starts out as an idea, like an egg. The idea hatches a conversation, through which the idea grows and changes shape, like a caterpillar. The conversation converges into specific test cases, like the formation of a chrysalis. These test cases contain what the software needs to do, and the software takes shape, enclosed by the story tests. Finally, working software emerges, like a beautiful butterfly. The cycle comes full circle after the software generates user feedback and new ideas. Most of the time, an Agile team has stories at each of these different stages in this life cycle.

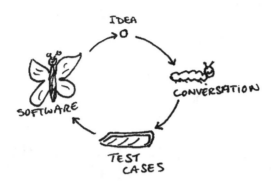

Help the team understand that a user story evolves from one artifact into another over time through conversation with the customer. They'll lose the benefit of user stories if they try to freeze them too soon. Encourage the team to keep asking questions to refine their understanding of what to implement.

Ron Jeffries summarizes three critical aspects of user stories as the 3Cs [Jef]:

Card: Writing stories on index cards to facilitate group conversations

Conversation: Asking questions and suggesting ways to split the story

Confirmation: Agreeing on what will be the tests used to assess whether the story is complete

Introduce the mantra "Card, Conversation, Confirmation" to the team to help them remember all three elements.

6.2 Encouraging Conversations

It's the conversations about user stories that enable the team to understand what needs to be built. These conversations need to be driven by developers and testers, checking with the customer that they have understood the story details as they implement it. Notice whether the team is struggling to work out what needs to be built, and remind them to ask the customer rather than guessing.

Other conversations will be about user stories for future iterations. These conversations are more often driven by the customer, who needs to get an early view on what can be developed when. She can't do this

Liz Says...

Get the Conversation Started

Be the catalyst for conversations between the team and the customer to check they're building the right thing. For example, if you find developers struggling to work out what the software should do, say something like this:

"Have you talked to Kate? She's our customer; maybe she can help work this out. Kate, have you got a minute?"

After the conversation gets going, you can slip away into the background. As the team gets used to having these conversations, they'll start happening without you playing the party host.

without help because she doesn't know the technical details and capabilities of the team. Encourage her to talk to the team to explore future stories.

Watch out that these early conversations about user stories aren't saved up until planning meetings; it wastes the whole team's time discussing stories that have not been thought through. Instead, suggest that new user stories are worked out in smaller groups with a customer and a couple of developers or a tester. Review these with the whole team later.

6.3 Working with Cards

We often find Agile teams using a computer with a projector in their planning meetings for capturing user stories. This kills conversations, because the team gazes up at the projector screen waiting for one person to update each story. Introduce index cards (or sticky notes) as an alternative way to record conversations about user stories. It's much easier to group stories on cards into iterations by moving them around on the table than it is to move rows up and down in a spreadsheet.

Start the team off by demonstrating how to use cards for stories yourself. Write each story you hear on a fresh card, and lay them out on

Rachel Says. . .
Rip It Up

Remember that the index cards reflect your current under-standing of the user stories. If after some discussion the story changes, don't be afraid to rip up cards you've been working on and create new ones.

I expect to see a few ripped cards every planning meeting. When I don't, then I'm concerned that the team is not engaging with their customer and not questioning whether the user stories presented could be sliced differently.

the table where they can be read by everyone in the conversation. Now anyone in the conversation can contribute by writing a new one.

Check that what you've written on the card captures what was said. If it doesn't, suggest that the customer correct or rewrite the card. As the story being discussed changes, add notes to the card, or tear it up and write a fresh card.

Demonstrate writing cards, and then stop.

As the meeting continues, stop writing all the cards yourself. When someone suggests a new idea, invite them to write their own card. You can say something like, "We don't want to forget that; can you write a card for that?" Or simply wait until someone else picks up a pen and does this without prompting. This happens quite naturally, because when several people are talking, one note taker can't keep up, and you'll soon find the team pitching in.

Put a stack of cards and pens in the middle of the table so anyone can write a card. We find that working with index cards on a table works only with small groups around a small table. For groups of more than five people, suggest shifting from a horizontal to vertical arrangement of cards. You can use sticky notes on a wall (or a portable team board), or you can post index cards on flip-chart paper pretreated with repositionable spray adhesive. Now the team can see all the cards without having to crane their necks or read upside down.

Make it easy for the team to use cards any time, not just in planning meetings. Have plenty of supplies available in the team workspace (rather then locked in a stationery cupboard), and get some card-organizing tools—CD boxes, plastic sleeves, binder clips.

Remind the team that these cards will end up on the team board and that the team will be referring to them in their daily standup, so it helps to use a consistent layout for the user **Use a consistent layout for story cards.** stories. Start with a short title at the top. Referring to them by reference numbers, as we've seen some teams do, makes conversations about the stories difficult to follow. Write the title legibly using a marker, large enough that it can be read by the team without having to walk right up to the board to decipher it. It also helps if the team gets into the habit of putting estimates (see Section 7.3, *Sizing the Work*, on page 91) in the same place on the card, such as writing them in the bottom-right corner.

Story Templates

When a team is new to user stories, you can recommend they use a story template such as this:

"*As a*. . . user, *I want*. . . capability *so that*. . . benefit."

Here's a filled-out example:

"*As a* book buyer, *I want* to see customer book reviews for a book *so that* I can decide whether to buy it."

This template helps the team remember to clarify who the user is and what the benefit of developing the story is.

The team needs a good understanding of the different types of users so they can fill out the *As a* part. You can suggest that the team create a stakeholder map or develop profiles with photos for typical user personas. It's even better arrange for the team to go out and meet real users in the setting that the software will be used in.

We have come across teams that religiously use a story template without really getting to the actual end user of the story. They try to force everything they work on into the story template, writing stories like "As a developer. . ." or "As an XML feed engine. . ." Explain that if there's no user interaction, then using this template may not help the team understand the requirement better, so there's no need to use it.

Remind the team that the purpose of a story template is to help the team learn to ask questions that improve their understanding rather than a form to be filled in. Once the team is used to working with user stories, the team can drop the story template. A short title is enough, and any other notes on the cards are simply reminders of the conversation, nothing more. Whether the team uses a template or not, always write the user story in language that can be understood by the whole team including the customer.

After the stories have been implemented as working software, the team relies on the tests, not the cards, for details about the story. They could throw cards out, but sometimes looking at the original card can jog memories about the conversation when it was created; this can be useful if the team needs to add more related stories in later iterations. Most teams we work with keep bundles of cards from past iterations for this purpose, but they don't often refer to them.

6.4 Confirming the Details

Once the team understands the basic story, who the user is, and what problem they're trying to solve, the team needs to discuss the details and agree on what behavior to implement. Work with the team to pin down the scope of each story as a set of tests that need to pass for the story to be considered "done." These *story tests*[1] help the team clarify what needs to be built and how much work needs to be done.

Story tests start life as bullet points scribbled on the back of a story card. Advise the team this is enough detail until the point that the story is planned into their next iteration. Later, these notes are used during the iteration as the basis for writing runnable test scripts.

We find that teams sometimes expect the customer to come up with these tests all on their own. Help the team understand that this is unlikely to work; a businessperson will often think only about what to do when everything is running smoothly rather than what can go wrong. For example, when thinking about how a search for a book works, they're likely to be more focused on what the user can do rather than what happens if there are no results to show.

Watch out when the word *test* comes up; your customer may look for an excuse to make a sharp exit, because this word gives the impres-

---

1. Another common term for story tests is *acceptance criteria*.

sion that a technical conversation is about to start. Rather than scaring them off with technical language, suggest the team draws out story tests by walking through some real examples. Examples help the team check that they understand what the software has to do and what behavior will meet customer needs. Examples also lead the team to explore situations that might need error handling.

Start by walking through a simple user interaction where a user achieves their goal. Now encourage the team to ask their customer questions like these:

- What data does the user enter?
- What does the user expect to see?
- Are there business rules that we need to be aware of?

Sketches of the user interface may help; rough pencil drawings are fine. It's the content and interaction that the team needs to understand, not the appearance.

Now prompt the team to ask about what could go wrong. What input data needs to be handled? Consider bad data and realistic quantities. During this exploration, remind the team that they're not writing test scripts, so you don't need to work out every single boundary condition just yet.

Here are some story tests for the user story: *As a shopper, I want to find a book by title so that I can buy it.* This uses a simple story test template *Given-When-Then* [Nor06].

- *Given* the user is viewing the search page and enters "Agile Coaching" (which has only one match), *When* the user clicks the Search button, *Then* full book details (title, author, picture of the book jacket, synopsis, price, reviews) and the Add to Shopping Cart button are shown.
- *Given* the user is viewing the search page and enters "Test-Driven Development" (which has multiple matches), *When* the user clicks the Search button, *Then* a list of book summaries (title, author, and price) are displayed, in price order with a Show More button next to each summary.
- *Given* the user is viewing the search page and enters "Waterfall Coaching" (which has no matches), *When* the user clicks the Search button, *Then* the message "Sorry, we can't find that book." is displayed.

If there are only a few tests, then jot the tests on the back of the story card. Or add them to a separate card and clip it to the story card. Watch out if a story has a big wad of tests clipped to it; this is a sign that the story is getting too big or the team is getting into too much detail.

Let's see how a team works out what the story tests are.

Working Out Story Tests

Amanda is a product manager who's taken on the role of the customer for a online bookseller. At the daily standup, she asked for input from the team on how difficult it would be to add ISBN search to the existing website. Damian and Larry, a developer and a tester, respectively, have volunteered to take a look at story details with her so they can give an initial estimate on the story.

"Why would users need ISBN search?" asks Damian. "They can already search by author or keyword."

"It came up in our last round of usability testing," Amanda explains. "It seems some users are in a hurry and don't want to wade through our search menus."

Damian frowns. "Shouldn't we be redesigning how search works then? I suppose this is a quick fix while we work out how to do that." Amanda nods and writes this story card.

> **BOOK SEARH BY ISBN**
>
> As a potential book buyer
> I want to find a book by entering an ISBN
> So that I can go straight to the book without wasting time.

Next, they move on to discussing the implementation of an example. Entering an ISBN like 1934356433 should display a book result page. The template for this already exists on the site, so there's no need to get into what details to display. Damian writes this story test.

STORY TEST ①

GIVEN user is browsing front page or any catalog page

WHEN user enters valid ISBN and selects SEARCH

THEN BOOK page is displayed showing standard fields

Note: valid is 10 or 13 digit with or without hyphen separator

Damian asks, "What should happen if the user hits Search without entering the full ISBN? Do you need a partial ISBN match?"

Amanda thinks for a moment. "Not really, that misses the point of the story. Can we direct them to our standard no results page with the top three Hot Picks?" Damian writes a second story test card to cover this.

Larry, the tester, reads it. "We need to handle thirteen-digit ISBNs too?" Amanda nods, and he adds a note to the bottom of the first story card.

"Do we return results only if they just enter the digits? What about whitespace and hyphens?"

"Sure." Damian adds, "It's not going to be much work to strip out blanks and hyphens, so we might as well throw that in too."

Amanda agrees, "Good idea."

The team members are now all happy that they understand this user story enough to give an estimate.

This story shows how some tests that come up get added to the user story while other story tests may be deferred.

User stories are a simple technique that a team can use for understanding their customer through talking about what users need. As a coach, your focus is to wean them off bad habits developed in pre-Agile days of accepting requirements to be implemented to the letter rather than asking why and offering alternatives. Show them how to use cards, and encourage them to get involved in conversations about user stories to offer their ideas and to draw out more details as story tests.

6.5 Hurdles

The following are some hurdles you may encounter.

No User-Facing Functionality

User stories are most effective when they are used to describe requirements of real human users. If you are working on a project to rework infrastructure or architecture, then there's often no obvious user-facing functionality to describe.

The template *As a... I want... so that...* is unlikely to be useful. But the questions "Who wants this? And why?" continue to be relevant for understanding how to prioritize the work. The team can still have a conversation about the problem being solved, the benefit to be delivered, and the story tests that will confirm they have delivered the story.

User stories can also be used to wrap a bunch of technical tasks into a more meaningful description, which makes it clearer to customers and management what's being worked on in each iteration. If work is described in the technical language of developers with references to libraries and code elements, they can sound completely cryptic to a customer.

Here's an example. The following description of some infrastructure work does not convey much about why this is needed. "Install WIBLv2 on Fred," where WIBL is a code library and Fred is a web server. Suppose the reason that the software is being updated with WIBLv2 is to handle different character sets for the Asian market. If we rewrite it as a user story, "As product manager, I want to see book information displayed in Asian character sets so we can sell our books into Asian markets," it makes the reason for doing the work clearer. The original description, "Install WIBLv2 on Fred," is a task to implement this new user story. This new user story should also lead the team into working out what tests need to be run to prove the story.

Requirements Must Be Documented

Some organizations mandate that software requirements are formally documented, usually because they are in a regulated industry and must show that they follow a process that can be audited. Or sometimes this information is needed to support a handover to another team, such as an operations team.

You can still work from user stories, but now you need to document them. A quick way to create an electronic record of stories is to take a digital photo (or a photocopy). You may also want to record any sketches drawn on whiteboards during the user story discussion. If you need more complete documentation, it can be written after the user story conversation.

Another approach to creating documentation that can't get out of step with the code is to write story tests as executable requirements using a test framework like FIT.[2]

Team Can't Meet Up

Obviously cards and sticky notes don't work for conversations between team members in separate office locations. You can still use user stories as the basis of conversations about user needs and discuss what story tests will be used to confirm the story has been implemented. Instead of using index cards, do the simplest thing that will work. For example, you can use desktop sharing software (such as NetMeeting or WebEx) so that teams in each location can see the same screen. Then use some basic software that allows you to write virtual sticky notes instead of index cards.

6.6 Checklist

- Teach the team the "Card, Conversation, Confirmation" mantra to help them remember that a user story has three essential elements: a conversation, a card, and a confirmation. Encourage the team to refine each user story through conversation with the customer.
- Show the team how to write story cards by doing it yourself and then stopping to make room for the team to write them instead.
- Make sure cards or notes are available in the team space and in meetings to discuss stories.
- "*As a. . .* user *I want. . .* capability *so that. . .* benefit" can be a useful template for user stories. Watch this does not become a form-filling exercise; such templates should prompt the team to ask questions. Once they're asking the right questions, the team can drop the template.
- Support the customer in working out details of stories before planning sessions. It helps shape the user stories if you get a few team members involved; they can ask questions and suggest story tests.

---

2. http://fit.c2.com/

Chapter 7

Planning Ahead

No one likes long meetings, but some in-depth conversation is required to make a realistic plan. So, how can you help the team strike the right balance in planning meetings?

Encourage the team to create plans of different granularities. They are likely to need both a rough plan that looks a few months into the future and a more detailed plan for their next iteration.

Planning is like cooking your favorite stir-fry vegetable dish:

Prepare: Work with the team—especially the customer—to get the user stories ready before the meeting. Slice the stories down as fine as you can without losing sight of the benefit.

Fry one at a time: Have one conversation at a time. If the team is talking about how to develop a story and then gets sidetracked by how important that story is compared to another, they can go round in circles.

Keep stirring: Keep the meeting flowing, and refocus conversations to prevent them from getting stuck.

Control the heat: The team may be under pressure to commit to more work than can be finished in the iteration. Help them work through the design details so they can give realistic estimates that take their past delivery rate (velocity) into account.

The secret of this recipe lies in the preparation.

7.1 Preparing for Planning

Encourage the team to work with the customer to get the user stories ready well before the planning day. We're not suggesting the whole team has a preplanning meeting; this can be done by a couple of team members.

Now guide the team through the following basic steps to create a plan:

Understand priorities:
Start with a team conversation about the user stories the customer would like to get in the next iteration to release.

Size the work:
When the stories are understood, help the team work out what needs to be done to deliver the stories.

Agree on the plan:
Wrap the meeting up by getting agreement on what can realistically be delivered.

A team that has a good understanding of what needs to be done can crank through all of these steps in less than an hour, whereas a new team working on a complex problem is likely to need more time. When you see that the team has a lot to work through, suggest each step is broken out into a separate meeting.

Work with the team to create an agenda for their planning meetings ahead of time. If everyone on the team knows what's happening and when, they can prepare properly. An agenda also comes in handy during the meeting. When team conversation drifts, you can refocus it by reminding the team about the agenda.

7.2 Understanding Priorities

Recommend that the customer opens the meeting by explaining her goal for the next iteration or software release. She presents the user stories and how each of them supports this goal. Ask her to rank the stories by laying out the cards on the table from the most important to the least important. Let the customer know you appreciate that *all* the user stories are important, but also set the expectation that it may not be possible get them all done in this next iteration.

Encourage the rest of the team to ask questions and look for opportunities to split the user stories down further. When stories are small

Rachel Says...

No Projector

Don't use a projector when working with user stories if you can avoid it. There's nothing more depressing than sitting in a meeting with everyone staring at the screen waiting for one person to type. It may seem like you're saving time because there won't be anything to type up after the meeting, but this is a false economy because it comes at the cost of valuable team time.

Instead, work with the customer to ensure they are prepared and they bring user stories on index cards to the meeting.

You can update any electronic records with the outcome of the meeting *after* it's finished.

I'm not saying *never* use a projector. They do come in handy if you need to look up existing user interfaces and designs in the meeting.

with clear story tests, they're easier to estimate and more likely to be delivered. However, if they're broken down too small, stories cease to be meaningful chunks of functionality from a business perspective.

Now prompt the team to review the tests for each story that's likely to be in the next iteration. A simple way to do this is to ask each team member to pick a story and read the tests aloud. You want the whole team to be aware of these tests so they take them into consideration when sizing the work.

7.3 Sizing the Work

Before they can estimate the work, the team needs to discuss software design implications. Make sure the team takes some time to dig into the technical details of each story.

Suggest the customer steps out.

This part of the meeting is probably not a great use of the customer's time. Let her know that it's fine to leave the meeting and you'll call her back later when the team has estimates on all the user stories. This will help the team too, because having someone visibly waiting for a conversation to finish can put pressure on them to wrap up their discussion prematurely.

Not Just Numbers
by Rachel

I worked with a project manager, Amir, who said in frustration to the team during a planning meeting, "Come on! I just want to get the numbers on the stories."

Amir gave the team the false impression that planning is about creating artifacts for project management. He was missing the important point that planning is about working out *what* to do, and that must come before working out how long it will take. The team cannot just "put the numbers on the stories" without having a conversation about what they need to do, and very often this discussion involves talking about the design of the software.

I shared my observation with Amir after the meeting, and he was glad I pointed it out. The next time, he made sure there was time in the agenda for some technical discussion. However, it took a while before the team built up the confidence to really talk about their design ideas as part of planning.

Encourage the team to use a whiteboard to help everyone visualize design options. There's no need for every last detail of the design to be pinned down in planning. Design decisions that don't affect the estimates (or impact work on other stories) can be left to the developers who end up working on that story.

Team Hates Planning
by Rachel

I worked with one team that hated planning meetings. The meetings dragged on for the whole afternoon with no breaks. Planning was dominated by the team leader, Amy, who attempted to nail down the design for all the stories before the iteration started. Creating the tasks for every story felt like micro-management of the work to the more experienced developers because this left them with very little choice about design by the time they got to building the software. Even worse, she usually cajoled the team into agreeing to estimates that were way below their original suggestions.

Rachel Says...

Keep Design Discussion Alive

I've met teams that formed an impression that the only meetings they should have if they're Agile are the "Agile meetings" (planning, daily standup, demo, and retrospective). This is just not true. Encourage the team to have meetings to talk about software design as needed rather than trying to cram these discussions into planning sessions.

The team brought up their concerns about these long planning meetings in a retrospective. The next day someone brought in a kitchen timer, which could be used by anyone in the meeting to timebox further discussion to ten minutes. After a while, if someone even reached for the timer and set it running, this was taken as a signal to wrap up discussion and move on.

Decomposing into Tasks

For large stories, which will take more than a couple of days to build, suggest to the team that they decompose the work into tasks: small pieces of work that contribute to the delivery of a user story (a few hours work not, more than a day). Doing this can sometimes reveal more story tests and ways to split the stories down even further. However, if the team already has a clear idea of the work, decomposing into tasks may be overkill.

There's another benefit for the team in breaking the work down into tasks. Small tasks make it easier for the team to share the work and coordinate their efforts so several people can work on the story. The team can post these tasks on their team board so they can see how much progress they're making every day. There's no special template for writing tasks, but they should be legible from a distance, ready for the team board.

When we don't know the codebase the team is working on, it can be tricky to lead conversations about what work needs to be done. Read

Liz Says...

Don't Play the Secretary

Don't take on all the writing in the meeting. It can be tempting to start doing this, because this is one thing you can do to support the team. But it stops everyone else from engaging in the meeting and can make it feel like the meeting is for your benefit rather than the whole team's. Encourage everyone on the team to get involved.

the story to the team, and then ask what needs to happen. Wait for the team to come up with ideas themselves.

If they get stuck, nudge them along by asking questions like these:

- Will we need any database changes?

- How are we going to test this?

- Do we need anything from other teams like editorial copy or GUI design assets?

- Is there anything else we need to do to meet our definition of "done"?

Estimating, Not Guessing

Once the team has worked out what needs to be done, they need to estimate how long the stories will take to complete. They do this collaboratively, without deciding who will work on which tasks at this stage. Ask the team to consider the work to be done *without* padding the estimates to allow for things to go wrong. Even if some days there seems to be one interruption after another, it's just not possible to estimate interruptions.

Be clear in the meeting that estimating is not making a wild guess! If the team really has no idea about what needs to be done (because they don't know the codebase or some new technology is being used), advise them not to jump into estimating and instead take time to explore what needs to be done. Some teams run their planning so that user stories are presented in the morning and estimating is done in the afternoon. This allows developers some time to look into the code before getting together to discuss what needs to be done.

If a longer investigation is needed, suggest to the team that they plan a *spike*. A spike is a timeboxed investigation with the goal of producing an estimate for a user story rather than

Spike to get a better estimate.

producing code. Once the team has a better understanding of the work involved, they can reconsider the story for the next iteration.

Arriving at an Estimate

The simplest approach is to discuss each story and then agree on an estimate. This usually works for small teams of up to five people. When planning with larger teams, you'll notice that some team members stay quiet and don't join in the discussion. This might be because they lack confidence, or they may be happy to go along with whatever is proposed—either way, the rest of the team doesn't get to hear their opinion. You can bring everyone into the conversation by introducing Planning Poker (see the sidebar on page 97).

As each user story is estimated, the estimate is marked on the story card, and it's laid out on the table. Create a *story card matrix* by grouping story cards with similar estimates into columns, and order the columns from low to high so the team can see them all. This is shown in Figure 7.1, on the following page.[1] This helps the team keep their estimates consistent. Mike Cohn calls this *triangulation*: "When estimating this way, you do not compare all stories against a single baseline or universal reference. Instead, you want to estimate each new story against an assortment of those that have already been estimated." His book *Agile Estimating and Planning* [Coh06] is a great reference for information about estimating and making Agile plans.

7.4 Review and Commit

The next part of planning is grouping the stories into an iteration schedule that the team can realistically deliver. This is often the hardest part because usually some trade-offs have to be made.

---

1. Courtesy of Kerry Jones, who explains more at http://blog.livingroomarchitect.com/2008/08/story-card-matrix.html.

Figure 7.1: A STORY CARD MATRIX

Checking Team Capacity

Once all the estimating is done, the team needs to understand their capacity so they can plan an achievable number of user stories to deliver. After running a couple of iterations, the team will have some average velocity data that shows how much they are likely to deliver per iteration.

If the team is just starting out and doesn't have any velocity data yet, a back-of-the-envelope calculation is usually precise enough. For example, suppose the team has three developers, one tester, and a project manager (who pitches in on documentation tasks). They're planning to work in iterations of two weeks. They figure that they lose about two days per iteration to meetings and another couple of days on support, so they estimate roughly they can take on about thirty days of work per iteration. Then they remember that one of the developers has a couple of days of vacation booked, so they adjust the figure to twenty-eight days.

Planning Poker

Planning Poker (Gre) was originally described by James Grenning. To play planning poker, each person on the team needs a hand of cards to give estimates with. Each hand of cards contains a card for each number in the point scale the team uses for estimating, such as 0, 1, 2, 3, 5, 8, 13, and 21 plus a card to flag up a story as too big; mark this with ! or some large number like 99.

When a story is read aloud:

- Each team member makes an estimation by choosing a card from their hand and placing it on the table *face down*. This is done so estimates won't be influenced by other players.

- When everyone has played their card, the cards are turned over and compared.

- If the numbers are all the same, then this estimate is marked on the user story.

- But if players have voted for different numbers of points, the team now discusses why they think the work is difficult or easy, and then they vote again.

- If someone has no idea, then they can play a card with a ?.

Playing Planning Poker keeps everyone in the meeting engaged and helps the team not to anchor on the first estimate shouted out. Although Planning Poker can help speed up the meeting, that's not the main point. Expect quite a bit of discussion when the estimates diverge before the team agrees on a figure. This discussion is normally very useful because it brings out assumptions and ideas about what the story is and how to build it.

Remember that Planning Poker is just one approach to estimating stories. We often come across teams using it inappropriately for estimating small, well-understood stories as part of planning their next iteration. You'll find this technique is most relevant when creating forward plans for releases over the next few months and a customer needs to get early feedback on initial story sizes before the user stories have been fully bottomed out.

Remind the team to take care that they don't overload any specialists on the team. There's no point in filling the plan with Ajax work if only one person can do this. If knowledge bottlenecks are a consistent problem for the team, encourage them to plan in some learning tasks to broaden the skills of the team.

Laying Out Iterations

Lay out the story cards in the order that the development team plans to work on them. Put the highest-priority ones first unless there are risks, dependencies, or deadlines associated with particular cards—these will need to be explained to the customer. You can see in following photograph how cards can be organized into a high-level view of what stories the team aims to release in the next few months.[2]

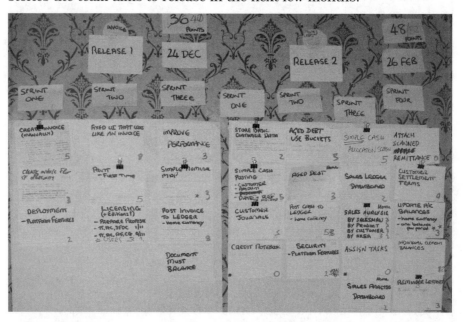

If the customer left during the estimating session, now is the time to invite her back in. Walk her through any changes made to the stories, such as splitting them down into smaller stories or new story tests. Now that the customer can see the estimates for the stories written on the story cards, she may need to reprioritize. Expect a little more shuffling of stories before making the final cut of what is and is not in the plan.

---

2. The photo is from a team applying Scrum, so they've labeled their iterations *sprints*. They ran an off-site meeting with all the senior stakeholders to create this plan.

Liz Says. . .

Be Realistic

However much the team or customer wants to get all the stories delivered, making an overoptimistic plan is likely to end in disappointment. It is important that the team plans for a sustainable pace so realistic expectations are set with the wider organization. Encourage the team to plan on completing the same amount of work as they completed last time—unless they know that circumstances will be different.

If the team feels particularly optimistic, then create a "backup board"—a queue of stories to work on if they finish early.

Looking Further Ahead

In an ideal world, the team would put a live release out to users at the end of every iteration, but there may be good reasons for releasing less often or for not always releasing to all users.

When filling up iterations in a plan that spans several weeks or months, remind the team that new stories are likely to come up. Encourage them to leave some wiggle room rather than packing the plan too tightly. The easiest way to do this is to leave one iteration unfilled. It's a space for new user stories and also a buffer that can help if development on any of the planned stories overruns.

It doesn't usually make sense to make a plan based on user stories that goes further out than three months. Beyond this point, use a road map based on story themes.

If the team is making only small changes to support live applications, rather than actively developing a product, there may be no benefit in getting the team together to create a longer-term plan. Instead, you might be better applying *kanban* (see the sidebar on the next page), which focuses the team on improving the flow of work.

Kanban by Karl Scotland, EMC Consulting

A kanban system for software development focuses on visualizing work as it flows through various stages of transformation in a value stream, with limits on work in progress at each point. This enables a team to see bottlenecks and constraints in the system, such that they can continually strive to improve the system and increase productivity and performance.

This focus on flow renders task estimates unnecessary, making breaking down tasks an analysis and design activity. Prioritization, planning, and releasing still occur regularly, forming a natural cadence around each activity. The team no longer estimates what it will deliver within a timebox, instead forecasting how much will be delivered from known cycle-time and throughput information.

A team setting a limit of three features being in progress at a time will concentrate on maximizing the flow of those features to completion, while deferring time spent on new features until they have spare capacity. The prioritization, analysis and planning of new work is therefore triggered "just in time," as opposed to being scheduled with an iteration planning meeting. Prioritization is based on the team's previous capability to deliver features, weighed against future business goals and objectives.

Kanban is the Japanese word for "visual card" and is used as a tool in the Toyota Production System. A kanban system for software development will often use an index card as the token limiting work in progress, and a token might represent a unit of value such as a user story. A kanban system is, therefore, able to manage the flow of single pieces of customer value through the development system from idea to release.*

---

*. Read more about Kanban at http://www.LimitedWIPSociety.org and http://availagility.wordpress.com/.

7.5 Keeping Track

After the meeting, the team will probably be itching to get started on the new stories. Before they scatter, someone needs to take responsibility for putting the stories and tasks up on the team board. Suggest the team nominates someone to be tracker—some teams rotate this role within the team.

We've noticed that putting tasks in a tracking tool can lead to micromanagement. There's no need to record all the tasks created in planning electronically; these will be tracked on the team board. Remind the team that stakeholders will be interested in whole user stories being finished rather than tasks because tasks aren't deliverables.

Tracking should focus on team deliverables.

It's also important to keep a version of release plans in software because it needs to be shared more widely with stakeholders. The team can simply list the user stories in a spreadsheet or on wiki page along with the estimates and when the stories will be delivered. The team will need to make sure that these different views of the plan are kept in sync.

Encourage the team to snapshot the planned stories along with the estimates. At the end of the iteration, they can compare this historic data with the velocity they actually achieved to work out their *hit rate*.[3] This is a calculation used by some teams we work with to help them see how accurate their planning is. For example, if the total story points planned is 50 and at the end of the iteration the estimates on completed stories add up to 40 points, then this team's hit rate is 80 percent.

7.6 Hurdles

The following are some hurdles you may encounter.

Customer Doesn't Know What They Want

If the customer has not prepared for the meeting, then the first part of the meeting may take quite a while to work out the user stories. It may help to hold a preplanning meeting with a smaller group of people to get a rough cut of stories before the meeting. This works best if you include at least one person from the team who can give some input from a technical perspective to verify whether the stories are feasible and not too big to deliver in a single iteration.

---

3. Introduced to us by Mike Lowery.

The Team Is Asked to Overcommit

Sometimes, the team may be asked to commit to more work than it can realistically deliver. This often happens when the customer has a hard launch date and there's a lot of pressure on the team. If you see that the team is about to commit to far more than their velocity shows they're likely to achieve, warn them that there's a high risk that all the stories may not be delivered.

If the team insists that they can do this, make sure that they slice the stories down quite finely so that for each area of functionality they have something that they can deliver, even if it isn't the all-singing all-dancing version envisaged.

Yesterday's Weather
by Lasse Koskela, Reaktor Innovations

I once worked with a smallish startup that had gotten a lot of good publicity; there was a lot of talk about it being the next MySpace, and so forth. The customer was the founder of the company who had built the first version of their online service himself in the wee hours over a couple of months. He was very much committed and enthusiastic to see the company go big.

After a few months of scrambling together a team and starting to rebuild the service for the needs of the world market, they decided to adopt Scrum—their incumbent ad hoc method was already showing its weaknesses. More discipline and visibility was needed.

Starting their second iteration, having delivered 25 points worth of features in the first iteration, the team was talking about trusting "yesterday's weather." The customer, however, was optimistic about the team's potential and managed to pitch the team to take on 35 points. They committed to 35; they delivered 24.

Again, the customer pulled a pep talk at the iteration planning meeting, pointing out how we were "just starting" and how the team was learning and improving all the time. The team committed to 35 and delivered 25.

Fourth iteration, same thing. They committed to 35 points because the customer "knew they could do it" and delivered much less.

At this point, the customer finally accepted what I and another coach had been trying to explain—the team's productivity will not improve by wishful thinking and "trying harder." At worst, it plummets under excessive pressure.

Plan Changes During the Iteration

Be on the lookout if the tasks on the team board change radically in the first few days of every iteration—this is a clue that planning meetings are probably being rushed. We've seen teams going through the motions of planning, listing tasks, and estimating them without really thinking through what needs to happen. Then when work actually starts on the story, it becomes apparent that the tasks on the board don't actually reflect the work that needs to be done.

Expect the team to create some additional tasks for a story as their understanding of the problem grows, but watch out if the tasks change a lot—that is a sign that the team didn't come to grips with what needed to be done in planning. Encourage the team to allow more time in their next planning session to work through the tasks, and also encourage the team to plan in some spikes.

Meeting Has a Lot of Conflict or Tension

Running planning meetings can be challenging. Developers often have opposing views on how the design should be done. Customers may not see the point in changing or splitting the stories.

Tension in the first part of the meeting, where stories are being discussed, may be about how to slice the stories or which are the most important stories. Encourage the team to explain their ideas and concerns to the customer. Be clear to the customer that they need to listen. Ultimately what stories end up in the plan has to be a joint decision.

The second part of the meeting can also become tense, because the team has to agree on how they will build the software to deliver the stories. A certain amount of conflict here probably helps test and improve ideas, but too much conflict is just unpleasant and inefficient.

If several alternative solutions are proposed, all of which seem equally good (or equally bad), then remind the team to judge each solution on how simple they will be to develop. The team might try developing both solutions. This will help them learn more about the problem. Soon it should be obvious if one solution is better than the other or if a combination of both ideas is best. Although it appears wasteful to code two solutions, it may well be the quickest way to learn, and it may provide a better solution.

Team Velocity Drops

It's pretty normal for the velocity of a new team to take a few iterations to settle down into a reliable figure, but once it settles, the team should still keep tracking it. Team velocity often slows down a little as the project grows and the software supports more user stories. At the same time, the team may have become more optimistic as their confidence with Agile grows. Help the team notice any slowdown and try to work out the root cause, although this may take more iterations to pinpoint. In the meantime, plans should be based on the new measured velocity rather than continuing to plan with the old velocity, hoping the magic will come back.

Planning Doesn't Make Sense

You'll find that there are times when going through the ceremony of planning doesn't make sense, such as when several team members are out of the office, on vacation, or in training, or when the team has a lot of bugs to fix. Bug fixes can't easily be estimated because most of the work is detective work tracking down what's causing the problem.

Rather than waste time on planning iterations during such times, create a prioritized queue of work on the team board. Now the team can work their way through it and prioritize work for the day in their daily standup. Continue working on small stuff until the team is back or the bugs are cleared.

If this happens a lot, then consider moving to a kanban style of development, which doesn't depend on iteration timeboxes to limit work in progress.[4]

7.7 Checklist

- Create an agenda with the team for planning meetings, possibly breaking planning into more than one session. Show the team how to use the agenda in the meeting to refocus conversations when they drift.

- Remind the team to work with the customer before planning meetings to prepare the user stories.

---

4. Jeff Patton has a nice summary of the kanban approach on his blog at http://agileproductdesign.com/blog/2009/kanban_over_simplified.html.

- Make sure everyone has an opportunity during planning meetings to ask questions about the user stories.

- Encourage design discussions before estimating the work. These often flow better if the customer steps out of the meeting.

- Suggest the team do a task breakdown for any large stories. Tasks can be posted up on the team board along with the stories during the iteration to help the team coordinate their work. However, recommend to the team that it's more important to track completed stories than tasks.

- Help the team estimate consistently by creating a story card matrix that groups stories with the same estimate together.

- Take care that the team works at a sustainable pace and doesn't make promises that their velocity shows they're unlikely to keep. Suggest the team check their capacity before making the final cut of what stories should be in the plan.

- Before the meeting breaks up, make sure that someone takes the cards and puts them up on the team board. The team also needs to take note of what stories are planned along with the initial estimates so they have a baseline they can use when calculating their velocity.

Make things visible to encourage the team to take responsibility.
▶ Guiding principle

Chapter 8

Keeping It Visible

What tricks do you use when you have to remember to do something? Whether it's collecting your shirt from the cleaners or posting a birthday card, we bet you make a visible reminder, like a note on the refrigerator door. The team has lots to keep in mind: iteration plans, retrospective actions, and the state of the software. Coach them to keep the stuff they need to pay attention to visible.

Useful information should be visible to all and not hidden away in computers. Plans kept electronically are information fridges; they give up their information only when they are opened. Help the team set up a *team board* that radiates their plans for all to see.

A team board is more than a place to put the current plan; it's a reflection of the team and what's important to the team. They can show where they're headed by posting up their product road map, release plans, and designs. Lots of teams we work with also personalize their team board with cartoon strips, postcards, and team memorabilia, which helps establish a team culture.

8.1 The Team Board

Most teams divide their board into columns to indicate progress (as in this photograph). The team puts the cards on the team board immediately after planning and moves the cards across the board until they reach the Done column.

Here's how it works:

Stories

All the stories are placed here, in priority order from top to bottom.

Tasks

Tasks are put here, in swim lanes next to the story to which they relate.

In progress

When work on a task begins, it is moved into this column.

Awaiting QA

When all the tasks are complete, the story card is placed into this column, and the completed tasks can be discarded. Seeing a card here prompts a customer or a tester to check the work and confirm it meets the story tests.

If a problem needs fixing, move the story card back to the Stories column and create new task cards for the fix.

Done

The goal is to get all stories that are done over here. This column should steadily fill up over the iteration.

The team delivers value only when a whole story is complete. Encourage them to focus on getting a few stories all the way across the board at a time, rather than a scatter-gun approach where lots of stories are in progress.

Take care that the board is laid out so that it is clear and legible.[1] It loses its power if people can't read what's up there. Encourage the team to use a consistent format for cards and write story titles neatly using a marker so that they can be read by the team in the daily standup. If they don't have great handwriting, then they can use a computer to print out signs for the board.

Make the team board easy to read.

If the team doesn't have space to move cards along, suggest they use stickers to show progress on the cards. Completed cards gather a series of overlapping sticky dots like a caterpillar (as shown).

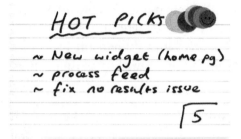

Not Started

All cards start with a red sticker on them.

In Progress

When work starts on a card, eclipse the red sticker with a yellow sticker.

In Review

When the task is being reviewed, cover the yellow sticker with a blue one.

Done

When the task is done, cover the blue sticker with a green one. If any bugs are found, show that the card is now work in progress again with a yellow sticker.

Use large, bright stickers so it's easy to see the status from a distance. Create a key explaining what the different color stickers mean—now it's easy for anyone to interpret the board.

---

1. See http://www.xqa.com.ar/visualmanagement/2009/02/visual-management-for-agile-teams/ for some tips on visual management.

Who's Working on What?

The beauty of a team board is that it enables the team to choose their own work. Nobody waits to be told what to do. They simply choose the next task from the board. You'll notice this encourages each team member to take responsibility for making the iteration a success rather than just focusing on "their" part. They can choose work that interests them without losing sight of everything that needs to get done.

To avoid treading on each other's toes, the team needs to know who's working on what. Although this gets discussed at the daily standup, it can change throughout the day. Make this visible by asking the team to tag the task they are working on with their name or picture. Now, if anyone needs to discuss that story, they can see who to talk to rather than interrupting the whole team. You can introduce a bit of fun by suggesting that the team create cartoon character avatars of themselves for this.

Tagging cards with who's working on them also helps make it more visible when someone gets stuck. Ideally, there should be exactly one task in progress for each developer (or pair). Look out for times when a developer has their name on multiple cards and explore why—it could mean there's a blocking issue or they need help. When a task is blocked, encourage the team to make this visible too. Do this with a brightly colored sticky note or by moving the card out of the In Progress area to a Blocked area.

Choosing Materials

You might assume that the team board should be mounted on the wall. We don't agree. Instead, create a portable team board that the team can bring with them to meetings. You can do this by using a whiteboard on wheels or a board made of light material, such as corkboard or foamcore.

The team board needs to be easy to use and interact with. You don't want cards to fall off if there's a slight draft. A magnetic board works well—the team can using magnets to hold cards onto the board rather than battling with pins or Blu-Tack. Keep spare supplies by the board—cards, stickers and magnets—so that it's easy for anyone to add a new task card. It's not your job to play board monitor for the team.

Board from a Box
by Rachel

A few years ago I worked with a team that had just relocated to new
open-plan offices. Each team was allocated an island of desks so they
could all sit together in project teams. There was plenty of funky furniture
but very few walls in the new space. Some temporary walls had been
provided for teams to use as meeting space and keep any project artifacts
in. These "walls" were made of rather flimsy polycarbonate sheets—it was
not easy to stick index cards to them with Blu-Tack, because the walls
had a tendency to fall over when you touched them.

Our team needed to create a team board, ideally one that we could see
from our desks and not hidden away behind a wall. Without a budget to
buy a board, our only option was to make one ourselves. Our ingenious
project manager, Oli, appeared the next day with a very large sheet of
corrugated cardboard, which we mounted with parcel tape on the outside
of the temporary wall facing our desks. To our surprise, we found that
corrugated cardboard is perfect for pinning index cards to. You can see
the result in the photo.

That's not the end of the story. After we had been using the board for a
few days, we were officially asked to take it down by someone from the
locations department because it was making the office look untidy. We
were noisily defending our right to keep the board when Darren (the VP of
engineering) intervened. He'd noticed our board and liked the fact that he
could see our progress on it. We were allowed to keep our tatty board. The
board was used for a several months more—the team members even took
it with them when they moved over to the next building (while the new
board that had since been ordered for them remained unwrapped).

Liz Says...

Agile Planning Software Won't Help

If there are problems in your project or Agile process, it is unlikely that introducing software to track the work will solve it. Using such software tends to bury problems and encourages poor communication practices such as creating stories for bugs without discussing them or making them visible.

It's far more energizing for the team to radiate their progress to the next release date on their team board. The team board is owned by the team and can be customized by them, whereas planning software is often owned, customized, and even maintained by one person.

Involve the team in choosing materials.

It's worth getting good-quality supplies. Brightly colored, super-sticky notes work better than cheap ones that are drab and drop off the board after a day or so. Involve the team in choosing the materials for their workspace by taking them on a trip to the local office-supply store at lunchtime.

Electronic Boards

You may be tempted to use software to create an electronic board, rather than use a physical board. Some teams we've worked with even beam their electronic board onto a wall in their workspace with a projector. We find electronic boards aren't as effective as a physical team board. People like tangible things, and cards are easier to interact with in a group than electronic data. Without the physical constraints of a team board, electronic boards tend to get overcomplicated.

If the team doesn't all sit together, then there is a practical reason for using an electronic board. Also, when the team is contributing to a program of work being implemented by multiple teams, the big picture covering all the teams may need to be maintained electronically. In either case, team members who sit together will still benefit from having a team board in their workspace.

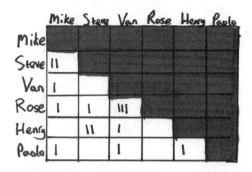

Figure 8.1: A PAIRING LADDER

If you have both electronic and physical boards, then both views need to be kept in sync. There's no need to duplicate the whole team board in software. Task-level information is not usually relevant after the iteration. All you need to do for electronic tracking purposes is write up the story titles with the story estimates agreed in iteration planning. Then, at the end of the iteration, note which stories have been completed, and record the team velocity.

Track completed stories, not tasks.

8.2 Big Visible Charts

Work with the team to design a "big visible chart" to increase the visibility of issues they want to track and then post it on the team board. This makes it easy for the team to see whether they're improving. For example, if the team agrees in their retrospective that they want to encourage pair rotation, they could use a *pairing ladder* to show who's paired with who and how often (see Figure 8.1). This information will encourage developers to pair with someone new every day.

Notice whether information on the charts is still giving useful feedback to the team. For example, suppose a team had a problem with long build times. They start working on tasks to bring the time down and create a visible chart of build times. The build time decreases. Do they still need to keep the visible chart? Maybe now they can automate the tracking. They can set up an early warning

Retire charts when the problem has gone.

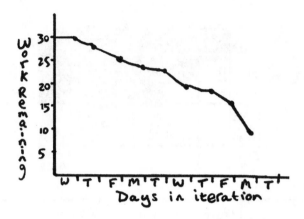

Figure 8.2: HAND-DRAWN BURNDOWN CHART

system to log build times, run a script to parse the log, and then send out an email alert if it exceeds ten minutes.

Note that as a coach, you need to take care introducing visible charts—get the permission of the team first.

Burndown and Burnup Charts

You've probably come across burndown charts. A burndown chart shows how much work is left to do in the iteration. For an example, see Figure 8.2. This gives a crude indication of whether the team is confident that they're on track.

What makes burndown charts a pain is updating them. If the burndown chart is stored electronically, the team needs to update time left in software (usually a spreadsheet) to generate the new burndown. You can guess how likely it is that every team member will conscientiously go do this every morning before daily standup.

We find most teams prefer to "burn down" estimates on the task cards by crossing out the old estimate and putting in the new one at the daily standup. Then one person can update a hand-drawn burndown chart on the team board based on today's total of work remaining. Following this routine helps the team to be more aware of whether they're likely to get all the stories done. Anything that has affected the development effort, such as missing team members, can be noted on the chart as

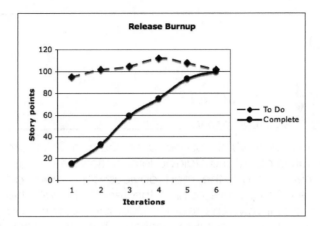

Figure 8.3: RELEASE BURNUP

well. This burndown chart can be reviewed at the end of the iteration (in either the demo or retrospective meeting) and then discarded.

What is often more useful is a *release burnup* chart that plots the number of complete story points across the iterations to the next release (as shown in Figure 8.3). The team updates this as each story is completed, which keeps the team's progress toward the release visible to everyone.

In Figure 8.3, the team plots story points complete against total story points left to do. The top line shows when stories were added or removed from the release. The bottom line shows how close to "done" they are.

Where there's a significant shortfall, the team needs to consider decreasing the user stories included in the next release. If it doesn't look like the team can deliver what they originally planned, make sure the team communicates this to the customer and any key stakeholders.

Measure the Right Thing
by Liz

One team I worked with tracked stories on their release burnup chart but marked them as "done" when the developer said it was finished, before it had been tested by a tester and checked by the customer. The whole team worked very hard to make sure that all the stories were built by the release date. However, the work to finish off the stories to completion wasn't visible on their release burnup chart.

Rachel Says...

Use It or Lose It

Don't make data visible just because you can. The team won't be bothered about maintaining information if it isn't used. The team members are the most obvious consumers, although there are often people outside the team who will check the team board. Involve the team in deciding what to track, and review whether it's useful to continue. If it's no longer useful, then take it down.

As the release date grew nearer, the list of outstanding problems grew and grew. The team was forced to prioritize which defects they were going to fix and which they were unable to do on time.

Eventually they did release—late and with less quality than desired, all because they tracked stories that the developer said was finished, rather than stories that *were* finished.

8.3 Maintaining the Team Board

Most of this chapter has been about the mechanics of setting up ways to make information more visible. There's one important aspect we haven't touched on, and that's keeping the data on the team board fresh. Stale data isn't useful.

You don't want to be working from "yesterday's news," so how does the information get maintained? Talk with the team about this. How can they solve this? The team can get together a few moments at the daily standup to update their board. Or they can take turns to sign up as tracker for the week.

Cleaning Up
by Rachel

I bumped into Matt one day. He was looking fed up. When I asked him how things were going with his new team, he sighed. His new team didn't seem to have any energy, and although there was a lot to get done, the team didn't seem to be engaged. I noticed that the team space had a air of neglect; it wasn't very obvious the team was working on a new project. I had a hunch that if we cleaned up, it might help. It would show the team that Matt cared about the new project and needed their focus.

The team board was quite small and scruffy. I suggested that the team could use a larger board. There was another board there that had been covered with the same writing for months. Matt tried wiping the old whiteboard with his finger, and the writing had been there so long that it didn't come off. But he didn't give up. He found some board cleaner and got started.

When I dropped by the following week, the team space was transformed, and Matt was looking a lot more cheerful. He found that after he got started cleaning up, the other team members helped him out. Having cleared the decks, the team now had a well-organized team board so everyone could see much better what needed to be done.

Notice whether the team board becomes cluttered or messy. It needs to be kept clear of cruft for the team to see everything clearly. We recommend the board is cleared at the end of every iteration. Then you can start your next iteration from a blank canvas.

8.4 Hurdles

The following are some hurdles you may encounter.

No Space for a Team Board

Often teams find it hard to find space for a team board. Be creative. We've worked with teams who used windows and cupboard doors for their team boards. You can also lean the board against a desk end if you don't have a free wall.

Team Doesn't Update Their Board

We often meet managers who bemoan that their team doesn't update the status of their team board and burnup chart. When we ask questions, it turns out that the board and burnup chart are not referenced in the daily standup or iteration demo. That's why the team sees the board as irrelevant to them and doesn't take the time to update it.

If the team doesn't keep the board up-to-date, ask them about it. They may be worried about letting the organization or customer know the true status of the project. Or maybe no one wants to be the "goody two shoes" who updates their own status. Take the time to look at the charts on the board, and talk with the team how they interpret what they see.

If they don't update the board, then their progress looks worse than it really is. Often you'll find that the team is actually working on the project but on tasks that aren't on the board. Ask them to add these new tasks to the board so everyone can see the real picture of who's working on what.

Concern That Cards Will Be Lost

Teams new to Agile often ask, "What if the cards get lost?" or the more extreme, "What if there's a fire?" You'll find that in practice this isn't a real problem. If a card does get lost, it can be re-created. You can keep a backup of the cards in any of the following ways: taking a photo of the cards, photocopying them, scanning them, or typing them up on the team wiki.

To avoid the mild inconvenience of losing a task, use the best materials you can to construct the board. For example, if you use sticky notes, then get the super-sticky ones.

8.5 Checklist

- Involve the team in designing and constructing a team board so they can make their iteration plan visible. This makes it easy for everyone to see what needs to be done and coordinate their work.

- It's the team's board, so they can use it to post personal stuff and charts that help them focus on improving the way they work.

- Find a board configuration that works for the team. Select materials that make it easy to read from a distance. If you use a color scheme, then provide a key to explain what the colors mean.

- Encourage the team to tag the cards they're working on with names or avatars. This helps make it more visible when someone is blocked.

- Don't bury information in electronic information fridges. However, if you have remote team members or the team is working as part of a large program, the team will need to create an electronic summary of their iteration plan.

- Use iteration burndown charts only as a crude measure of team confidence that they're on track. Encourage the team to update this themselves at the daily standup or by nominating a tracker. A release burnup chart will be a better indication of progress and helps the customer spot whether they need to descope or budget for more iterations.

- Clear the board at the end of the iteration. Review visible charts during the iteration, and retire them when the team no longer finds them useful.

Part III

Caring About Quality

Chapter 9

Getting to "Done"

Ever watched little kids playing soccer? They all chase after the ball rather than getting into a space where the ball can be passed to them or paying attention to defense. They don't know how to work as a team to score goals yet.

Agile teams need to learn how to work together to meet their goals. They are not kicking a ball; instead, they pass software between team members. Each person on the team plays a part in getting the work done.

To succeed, they must first understand what functionality to build and what testing needs to happen for each story. Then they need to work together to make sure that all of this gets done.

You'll find where they often come unstuck is underestimating how much time it takes to test the software and fix any problems with it. Help them get clear on exactly what being done means and how they can collaborate to make it happen.

9.1 Who Does the Testing?

Testing is not one person's job; it's the responsibility of the whole team. Every person on the team has different skills to contribute toward getting to "done." As their coach, you can help them work out how to coordinate their efforts.

Developers need to make sure their code passes the story tests before they release it for further testing. This avoids wasting the time of customers and testers who pick up the code for testing next.

Encourage developers to use their programming strengths to automate as much testing as possible, although they're unlikely to spot problems with software they just wrote.

Customers know most about the environment the software will be used in. Their focus is usually on whether the user can achieve the goal of the user story. Be aware that customers can miss edge cases, where the system needs to handle errors or odd data. Urge the team to make the latest working version of the product easily available for customers to try out any time.

Testers excel at destructive testing, thinking about edge cases where the system may be abused. They help the team flesh out story tests and verify that story tests are passing. Testers often need support from developers to automate tests. Watch out for opportunities for them to pair up on this.

External teams may carry out specialized testing before the software can be released, like security testing, usability testing, or platform testing. Recommend that the team include time for responding to problems found by this specialized testing in their release plans.

For these different roles to collaborate, they need a shared definition of what "done" means.

9.2 Defining What "Done" Means

Bring the whole team together to agree what their definition of "done" should be. Kick off the discussion with this basic definition.

"Done" means the customer is happy with what has been developed, *and* all the story tests pass.

Now ask the team what additional checks ought to be carried out per story before it can be considered to be "done." Encourage them to draw on their experience; their definition of "done" has to contain the checks that they think are important. Here's a list that you can use to prompt them:

- The code has been reviewed by another developer on the team.
- The code has unit tests.
- Automated tests have been created for the story tests.
- Exploratory testing has been done by a tester on the team.

Finish Card Checklist

UNIT TEST

AUTOMATED TEST

REFACTOR

SOURCE CONTROL

TEMPLATE / KEYWORDS

RELEASE

MooOOoOOoOOoOOo

STAGE TO PRODUCTION AS APPROPRIATE

Figure 9.1: EXAMPLE OF DONE CHECKLIST (CONNEXTRA, 2002)

- The user documentation has been updated to describe the new functionality.

- Performance testing has been carried out on a specified set of operating system configurations.

Write up their customized definition of "done" on a whiteboard where everyone can see it. Now review this with the team. Is there anything else that must be done before code is released? Listen carefully for any checks they assume happen later after the iteration ends. Ask them who will do that work. If it's the team, it probably should be included in their definition of "done." Once the team is happy with their "done" checklist, encourage them to display it prominently in their workspace.

We've included an example of a "done" checklist in Figure 9.1, which a team created to display on their board. Let's take a closer look at the checks on it. You'll see it includes obvi-

> Make the definition of "done" visible.

ous items such tests and refactoring; it also lists source control. We wouldn't normally include source control in a definition of "done," but this team had assets (images, templates, and data files of keywords) that they wanted to remember to check in. Developers celebrated each check-in of code with a toy cow that mooed—this was a signal for the other developers to pull in the latest changes. For this product, being "done" with a story was actually putting it into production. Encourage the team to look for slices of functionality that they can take all the way through to "done" during the iteration rather than at the end.

When's the best time to have the conversation with the team to define what "done" means? You can discuss this with the team at the start of the project, as part of a session to define working agreements for the team. Or you can leave working out the details until the team hits an iteration where some stories don't get finished. The team will probably revisit their definition of "done" in retrospectives, so expect it to evolve during the project.

As you'd expect, there are times when the definition of "done" does not apply. There's no need to apply "done" checks to *spikes*—throw away code being developed to learn about what's required or to see how a new technology might be applied. Remind the team about this at iteration planning time because this affects the estimates.

Once the team has a definition of "done," notice whether the team still struggles to get stories complete by the end of the iteration. If so, help the team see where the bottleneck is and look for ways to improve the flow of their work. You can do this by applying a kanban approach to set limits on work queues and reflect these on the team board (as described in the sidebar on page 100).

9.3 Planning in Testing

When the team is clear what has to happen, they're less likely to leave all the testing until the last day of the iteration. Take time in planning to talk with the whole team about what the testing tasks are. Don't let them get away with adding a single task labeled "Testing" for each story—this is a cop-out! A few examples of testing tasks are writing automated tests, preparing test data, and setting up environments.

Invite testers to share their concerns.

Testers are usually outnumbered by developers on the team, so they can get sidelined in meetings. Make sure testers are invited to planning sessions, and encourage them to play an active role. Watch that the team listens to their concerns. If they're frowning or disengaged, invite them to share their viewpoint.

Rachel Says...
Demonstrate Respect

I have sometimes been shocked at the way testers are treated on software teams. They're often left out of conversations about user stories and don't get invited to team meetings or social events. Look for ways that you can help all members of the team feel included.

If you hear people on the team make complaints using roles as labels, such as "the testers are never around," then take care not to join in. Instead, shift the conversation back to the situation the team currently faces and remind them about the pressures that people in those roles may be under.

By taking the time to listen to everyone on the team and showing an interest in their work, you demonstrate that you value them and their contribution to the project. When you show respect, you're likely to get respect in return.

The team will be in a better position to plan testing if they understand more about what testers actually do. Bring developers and testers to sit together in the team workspace; this improves communication, and seeing each other at work helps build mutual respect. You can also suggest that developers and testers pair up to work out details of story tests and to find the root cause of failing tests.

9.4 Managing Bugs

For the team to get all their stories to "done" by the end of the iteration, they need to be clear on how to handle bugs that come up during the iteration. It's pretty clear-cut that if a story test is failing, it needs to get fixed before the story can be considered as "done." But what should happen if the bug is a new story test that wasn't discussed in planning? Does the team fix the bug in the current iteration or defer it to a later iteration?

Help the team decide what to do by working through the options with them. If the software already delivers the main benefit of the user story, there may be a case for deferring the bug fix until later. However, if leaving the problem in the software prevents an imminent release, it may need to be fixed now. Because it's unplanned work, fixing it might put the team in jeopardy of not completing other stories. Remind the team to talk to their customer about the situation if they're worried this might happen.

Here's an example of a typical conversation that occurs when a developer checks whether they're "done."

Not Quite Done Yet

"Finally!" grins Rebecca. "I've finished the carousel story. It all works now." She looks round the office, keen to show it off. "Larry, are you busy? I need you to test this."

"Sure. I just need to finish this test, and then I'll be with you." Rebecca picks up an apple to eat while she waits for Larry.

"Right, what've you got for me?" he asks, spinning his chair around so he can see Rebecca's screen.

"I've finished the book carousel," she says proudly.

"Cool. Let's see it then."

Rebecca fires up the website and goes to the new book listing page. A 3D carousel of book titles spins around.

"I like it! How do you get it to stop on the book you want?" Larry asks. Rebecca clicks a book, and the carousel stops spinning.

"Can you do that from the keyboard?" Rebecca tries a few keystrokes with no luck.

"Nope, I'll need to look into how to do that." She scribbles on a yellow index card in front of her.

The next day Rebecca has fixed the problem, and Larry tests it properly as part of a clean build deployed to the integration server.

"Rebecca, it's pretty good now. There's just a couple of things I want to run by Amanda." Larry calls over to Amanda, "Amanda, have you got a moment?"

"Sure, if you make it quick. I have a meeting at 3." She smiles and walks over to Larry's desk. Rebecca joins them.

"I've just finished testing the carousel that Rebecca has been working on. But I'd like you to make a call on a couple of things I found." Larry turns to Rebecca and says, "Rebecca, do you want to show Amanda how it works?"

Rebecca opens up the new book listing page and shows Amanda the carousel. "That looks really nice. I like it!" Amanda says.

"Yeah, it looks great. Just a couple of small problems," says Larry as he reaches over for the mouse. "This is what it displays if we don't have an image for a book." And Larry spins the carousel to the back.

"Oh, that's not so good," frowns Amanda.

"What should we do about books that don't have an image? We didn't think about that when we estimated this story," says Rebecca.

"Don't display it in the carousel for now. Then we'll get a placeholder image created for those books," Amanda decides. Rebecca notes this as a task on a yellow index card.

"It also doesn't display long book titles very well in version 6 of this browser," Larry demonstrates.

Rebecca looks slightly disappointed that Larry has spotted another problem. "That's going to be tricky to fix; it works fine in Firefox and Safari."

"How long does a title have to be before it goes over the limit?" Amanda asks.

"Well, I saw only a couple as I was looking through. Let's see," and Larry copies one of the long book titles into an editor and gets a word count. "This is 98 characters, and it looks like it's been cut off at 95."

"Rebecca, can you find out how many books have titles longer than 95 characters?" asks Amanda glancing at her watch.

"Let's see," Rebecca says, furiously writing a database query. "Four."

"Four? Out of how many?"

"Just over 5,000 books."

"I can live with that. Don't bother fixing it this iteration. I'd rather you worked on the recommendations engine story."

"OK. I'll fix the problem with the missing images, and then tomorrow I'll be able to make a start on recommendations." Rebecca smiles, looking relieved.

> "Great! Well, I need to head off to my meeting now." Amanda grabs a report from the printer and then adds, "Maybe I'll catch up with you two for lunch if you fancy trying the new juice bar."

In our story, the team uses yellow cards for bugs so they stand out on the board as things that need to be fixed. You'll notice that the tester discusses only the borderline cases with the customer. The customer makes a decision to defer fixing the display of long book titles when she finds out that this affects only a few books. Our story does not say what gets documented about that bug, which leads us into the murky area of bug tracking.

Flagging Failing Tests

Discourage testers from burying bug reports in a bug tracker. Instead, encourage them to use the team board to flag failing tests, making them visible to the whole team. Now it's clear the team has more work to do before the story is complete.

> ### Bugs by Email
> *by Rachel*
>
> I recently worked with a team where one of the testers always communicated problems she found by emails that were also copied to the head of QA. The developers desperately wanted her to talk to them *before* firing off emails outside the team, especially because the developers didn't check their emails much while they were coding. Her reasoning was that she didn't want to interrupt them, and she was trying to keep the QA manager in the loop so they could justify getting another tester on the team.
>
> Unfortunately, the developers started bypassing her and deploying changes to live environments without her input. This was like pouring gasoline onto a fire! The head of QA called a workshop with the whole team so that the situation could be resolved.
>
> The team agreed that, going forward, the testers would flag problems found with stories visibly by posting colored cards on the team board. Developers would then annotate these cards with the build number that fixed the bug. This way, the tester would not interrupt the developers or bury problems in email.

Antony Marcano warns us that a bug tracker can turn into a hidden backlog (see the sidebar on the facing page). We like his advice to treat

The Hidden Backlog by Antony Marcano, testingReflections

I joined a well-established team that had been delivering working software every few weeks. During the iteration, we'd do exploratory testing whenever we thought the story was close to done. When we found bugs, we duly filed them in the bug-tracking system. Sometimes we'd go ahead and fix the bug, while other times we referred the decision to our customer.

We were using TDD, so before fixing each bug, we'd write an automated story test reproducing it. Doing this made me realize that these bugs were simply story tests that we hadn't previously thought of.

We were all getting frustrated that we had to write a bug report into the bug-tracking system and then essentially repeat the same information in an automated test—this felt wasteful. The only problem that the bug tracking was solving for us was tracking status and who was working on it.

I realized that if a bug report is analogous to a story test, surely I could summarize one or more bugs as a new user story. We already had a means of managing user stories! That's when it came to me that we were essentially working from two backlogs! One backlog of yet-to-be-implemented behaviors summarized by the user stories and another backlog of misbehaviors in the bug-tracking system! The bug-tracking system was in essence a *hidden backlog*.

The side effect of maintaining these separate backlogs is that we treated the bugs and the stories differently. We didn't prioritize them in the same way or at the same time. I've seen teams budget a fixed amount of effort to fixing bugs from previous iterations without prioritizing them against the stories in the current iteration or budget for fixing all bugs even if they were less valuable than stories on the backlog. Following this approach, we reserved time for fixing bugs regardless of their impact, which sometimes led to a bug being fixed that was less valuable than a new story, and vice versa.

Now, on new projects, I suggest creating a project in the bug-tracking system only when we need it. I've not found a need for one for quite some time.

bugs that are deferred as new stories, and add them to the backlog[1] of user stories for future iterations. No separate bug-tracking tool is required, although one may be useful to store details of a bug electronically, such as screenshots.

Remember, there's always more than one way to solve a problem. We also meet teams that avoid creating a hidden backlog by putting all their bugs and stories into a bug tracker, such as Trac,[2] and using the tracker as their planning tool. This solution requires a technically savvy customer who'll invest the time to learn how to use a new tool rather than sticking with more familiar office tools like spreadsheets.

Finding Root Causes

Every time a bug is found, there's an opportunity for process improvement. Encourage the team to work out what caused it and think about how this might be avoided next iteration. This can be done as each bug comes up or can be discussed in the next retrospective. We'll talk more about what developers can do to improve their code quality and reduce the number of bugs found in their code in Chapter 10, *Driving Development with Tests*, on page 137.

9.5   Getting Feedback Early

Early feedback can help nip problems in the bud. Developers often don't seek feedback early enough, which can lead to stories that don't get finished by the end of the iteration, and it also places an uneven load on testers. There's no need for a developer to implement a whole user story before checking they're on the right track. If they have a slice of the story ready, then they can make it available to their customer or a tester to get feedback on it.

> Encourage developers to seek feedback early.

You'll notice developers often put off conversations with the customer or testers until they're finished working on the story. In the story, we saw that Rebecca felt proud of her work and was disappointed when problems were found. No one likes making mistakes. It's only natural for developers to delay making software available for testing until they feel it's really polished. They may also be concerned that getting feedback too early will slow them down.

---

1. *Backlog* is a term used to describe a list of work to be done in the Scrum framework.
2. http://trac.edgewall.org/

Liz Says...

Stay Calm

Whatever the project pressure, try to keep calm yourself and not add to the pressure on the team unnecessarily. Your mood can rub off on the team and affect them even if you don't want it to affect them.

We find developers delay seeking feedback when they're worried that the tester will criticize what they've done. Notice how testers and customers present feedback to developers. Although a tester may relish finding bugs, it's important that any negative feedback is given in a way that developers will listen to. Share with them what you learned in Section 2.2, *Giving Feedback*, on page 23. Encourage them to share their observations rather than opinions.

Feedback is possible only if the person has time to give it. Notice if the customer is very busy and not often around. No one likes to interrupt someone who's obviously busy. Developers may feel like they're wasting the customer's time if they show anything less than the finished article. If the customer is not sitting with the team, ask them to find an hour every day to be available to help the team.

9.6 Recovering from Not Getting Done

We've been talking about how to improve the chances that the team will get to "done" for all of the stories by the end of the iteration. But what do you do if the team *doesn't* achieve this?

Take this seriously. Talk about what happened in the iteration demo and retrospective. Help the team understand why this happened, and ask for their ideas to prevent this from happening again. Also recognize that this is a problem that affects how much work the team can reliably commit to next time. Before the team plans the next iteration, they need to decide how not getting to "done" affects their velocity.

Rachel Says...

Be Patient

Helping a team make realistic plans takes time—be patient. The team has to recognize there is a problem before they'll be willing to change. It may take a couple of iterations before the team can really believe that they are overcommitting. They're always optimistic that things will be better the next time around.

If they're rushing and working long hours, they may be too immersed in building more software to think about this. You may need to think of a way to cause a breathing space, like an off-site meeting or social event, before you can really get through to them.

Don't just leave unfinished stories and tasks festering on the team board. Clearing the team board completely at the end of the iteration takes some of the weight off the team. These incomplete stories need to be reconsidered as part of the next iteration planning meeting, so take them along with the new stories.

We have encountered organizations where pressure for teams to say "yes" to everything that's presented to them is overwhelming. Even though they know in their hearts that they're overcommitting, they don't know how to avoid the train wreck they see coming. Your job as a coach is to convince them that saying "no" is an option. This becomes easier if the team says "no" rather than individuals saying "no." As a coach, talk informally to people on the team about their concerns. If they can put them into words talking to you, then this may help them to start talking about it as a team.

Help the team gather data to make the case for slowing down and committing to less. Remind them of their measured velocity when planning the next iteration; averaging velocity data over several iterations can make velocity figures more convincing. If they still decide to commit to more work than their velocity shows is likely to get done, make sure the customer knows there's a risk that not everything will be delivered.

If you cannot persuade your customer to drop any stories, you may be able to convince them to slice the user stories more thinly to increase the chances that the team delivers some of them.

9.7 Hurdles

The following are some hurdles you may encounter.

It's Not My Problem

We sometimes encounter individuals who have a rigid view of the tasks that are appropriate for them to do. You might have a developer or a customer on the team who insists that "testing is for testers." Or you may have a tester who says automated tests must be written by developers. The cause is likely to be fear of trying something new. Try to cajole them into trying to do some testing tasks, and make sure they have someone to buddy up with to support their learning.

Look for ways to build a sense of accountability for the whole team. You may get some shift in attitude if results of the iteration are very visible. We'll talk more about this in Chapter 12, *Demonstrating Results*, on page 171.

Working with Remote Testers

Sometimes testers are located in another office or even another time zone. You'll find this increases the delay in getting feedback from testers, which may reduce the amount of software that the team can get to "done." The team may be tempted to test the software in the subsequent iteration; this gives an illusion of progress and means that any bugs from the previous iteration interrupt development in the next iteration.

It may help to arrange a separate phone call meeting with the testers to get estimates of testing tasks in advance of iteration planning, so these can be considered alongside the development tasks. This will help prevent the team from committing to more work than they can get done.

Working with remote testers means that, besides email, the team will need to track bugs electronically. Make sure that everyone on the team has some easy means of interactive communication with remote testers, such as phone or IM.

Organization Mandates Use of a Bug Tracker

We have worked with organizations where the use of bug-tracking software is mandated for all teams. Bug rates are even derived from these tools to show that testers are adding value. As Mary Poppendieck says in *Implementing Lean Software Development* [PP06], the job of testers is to "*prevent* defects" rather than collect them. If a story is still on the team board, then any problems that must be fixed should be posted there too, where the whole team can see them. Recommend the team uses bug-tracking software only for bugs that are found after the iteration ends.

9.8 Checklist

- Define what "done" means with the team. Display this as a checklist in the team workspace. Include testing done by customers, developers, and testers, but exclude testing done outside the team.

- Make sure that testing is considered in iteration planning so testing tasks are understood by the whole team.

- Encourage developers to work closely with testers and their customers to get early feedback on stories. Ask the customer to reserve time every day to answer questions from the team.

- Recommend that software is made available to customers during the iteration. Encourage the team to look for slices of user stories that can be delivered early rather than waiting until the iteration ends.

- Use the team board to display bugs that need to be fixed before the end of the iteration. Instead of creating a hidden backlog in the bug tracker, ask testers to work with the customer to turn bugs that are deferred into new user stories that can be planned into future iterations.

- If the team doesn't get all the stories done, talk about why this happened with the whole team in the demo or retrospective. Clear the board at the end of the iteration, and take any incomplete stories into iteration planning. Help the team gather velocity data so they don't overcommit in the next iteration.

Chapter 10

Driving Development with Tests

We meet lots of teams that say they're Agile but that still rely heavily on manual testing. Developers toss software over the wall for testers to find any problems; then testers bounce it back again with copious bug reports. Days go by as developers and testers run around in circles trying to patch the software until it's good enough to deliver.

Encourage the team to reduce this stress by making the move to *Test-Driven Development*. The team can use automated tests to find out whether the code works—in minutes rather than hours or days. Now developers can be confident they're building on a solid foundation, and testers can focus on edge cases instead of wasting time on trivial problems.

Reaching this automated testing nirvana is one of the biggest challenges you'll face as an Agile coach. It's a complex change because introducing TDD requires solving technical, personal development, and teamwork challenges. Let's look at how to get started and how to overcome barriers to implementing TDD. Then we'll see how you can help the team make the shift to *Continuous Integration*.

10.1 Introducing Test-Driven Development

Allow plenty of time for the team to make a transition to TDD. It's likely to take a couple of months before they're really driving their code with tests. Your first challenge with implementing TDD is working out where to start. We recommend you pick off one problem at a time rather than attempting to introduce TDD in one big bang.

Test-Driven Development

Test-Driven Development turns automated testing up a notch; no code is added without first writing an automated test.

To drive code with tests, a developer starts by writing a test for the code she wants to write. She runs the test to check that it really does fail. Now she writes the minimum code to make the test pass. After each new test passes, she looks for opportunities to consolidate the code and eliminate duplication. She builds up the code by repeating these steps.

Developing code this way encourages a developer to think about solving one small problem at a time. It also helps the developer work from the outside in rather than the inside out—because for each test they consider the interface of the code before its internal logic. Because applying TDD drives the developer to make small design decisions as they go, it's also sometimes referred to as *test-driven design*.

If the team is starting out on a greenfield project, it can jump straight into full-blown TDD (as described in the sidebar on this page). Most teams, though, will be building on existing code that doesn't already have automated tests, so the first challenge is to figure out how to wrap automated tests around this legacy code. Ease the team into TDD; get the team members started writing a few automated tests a day before trying to drive their code with tests. This gives them time to build up their skills and testing infrastructure before they attempt to work test-first.

Spend time working with the team to understand the real state of the code, the level of experience of the team members, and how interested each of them is in making changes to the way they work. Now apply the PrOpER cycle (Section 1.4, *How to Start Coaching*, on page 11) to dismantle any barriers to adopting TDD.

The following story illustrates some typical challenges that you might encounter.

Introducing TDD Too Quickly
by Rachel

A couple of years ago, I worked with a team that appeared to be in a good position to try TDD. They were developing a content management system in Java. Their development manager had already arranged for developers on the team to take a training course so they could hone their skills in writing JUnit tests. He called me in to follow up with coaching the team in TDD. This request seemed pretty straightforward, but I didn't recognize what I was getting into.

On the surface, there was only one obvious technical challenge: the team had embedded calls to some third-party document management system in their code. They'd need to find a way to write tests without calling this library. This didn't seem insurmountable to me. I was confident that they could use *test doubles*[1] to stub out the library calls. But when you introduce TDD to a team, it's not just technical challenges that you need to solve. There are human challenges too.

I made a start by arranging a pair programming session with each developer on the team. My plan was to make a start by trying to write JUnit tests for the user stories on which the team was currently working. However, after my first day, I'd encountered a number of challenges that told me the team wasn't ready for TDD just yet.

The day started out well. I sat down to pair with Dom, the tech lead. He seemed pretty busy but was willing to try writing some automated tests. He'd just implemented a bug fix, so we decided to write a test to prove the fix he'd just made. When he ran our new test from the command line, he was surprised to see it fail—apparently he hadn't completely fixed the bug! The test data we chose in our unit test triggered a problem that he hadn't considered when he manually tested the code earlier. This experience seemed to convince him that writing automated tests for every bug fix *might* be a good idea!

I moved on to pair with Dave, who was working on some fairly straightforward code that parsed XML input files. He'd already gotten some unit tests running within Eclipse, and we added a couple more simple test cases. I was able to point him in the direction of a library of XML assertions that might be useful to him, but otherwise he didn't seem to need any help.

The next session was quite difficult. John was very new to Java, and he hadn't grasped some basic principles of object-oriented programming. He didn't know how to use his IDE to write or run unit tests. He was using one single main test method that he edited every time he wanted to check his code was working. He was also clearly struggling to understand how the existing system worked, but when I suggested we ask one of his team-mates, he balked. We spent an hour or so unpicking his long test method trying to extract some JUnit tests, but it really seemed a fruitless task.

---

1. See http://xunitpatterns.com/.

The last session of the day was with Chris, the only contractor on the team, and he was using yet another IDE, NetBeans. He seemed quite experienced but was concerned about the challenges of writing unit tests for code that directly called a third-party library. I mentioned the possibility of using mock objects, and he told me a developer who had recently left the team had been using mock objects in her tests. We opened up the tests she'd written, and they looked in good shape. However, it was a different story when we tried to run them. The code had moved on since she wrote the tests—they didn't even compile anymore! No one on the team had run the tests since she left. She might as well have never written them.

That's when it sank in. The "team" was not working as a team. They were working on different areas of the code with quite different ideas about how to write the tests. No one was running tests written by anyone else; they were even using different IDEs. There was no buy-in to adopting TDD or what that meant for the team.

Before they could get started with TDD, we needed to do some more basic things. The team needed to work together to establish a test strategy and to agree on how they would organize their tests into a shared suite that anyone in the team could run.

I discovered later that the reason the development manager wanted the team to adopt TDD was because the testers on the project were overloaded. They were finding trivial problems with the code, which could have been prevented by developers doing some basic testing of their own code. But the manager failed to communicate that to the team. They needed to hear it from him to understand why they were getting training and coaching in TDD and give them some reason to make the change.

Buy-in from the Team

As the story illustrates, teaching the team how to write tests isn't enough. The team has to make a shared commitment to write tests and to run them. They need some compelling reasons before they will commit to taking on the extra work of writing automated tests. Make sure that they understand the benefits of TDD and that they appreciate the drivers behind the change.

Get the team together to build agreement on what they can commit to. List the blockers that they see preventing them from making a start with TDD. Now ask them for their ideas for resolving these blockers. Use gradients of agreement (see Section 2.4, *Building Agreement*, on page 27) to determine which of the actions the team has energy to work on first.

Coding Dojo

A coding dojo brings developers together to work on a prepared programming challenge.* A coding dojo is a great way to improve developer design skills and encourage learning on the team. The approach was inspired by Dave Thomas's code kata.

Running a dojo is quite simple. Choose a coding challenge or kata.† Selecting the challenge ahead of time allows participants to prepare for the dojo.

The dojo starts with two developers working on the challenge at a computer at the front of the room. The computer is hooked up to the projector so everyone can see the code as it's being written.

As the developers work on the challenge, they talk aloud explaining what they're doing and giving a running commentary on how they are solving the problem. If the group can't follow what's being done, then the pair must pause to explain.

To keep everyone involved, one half of the pair is swapped out every five minutes and is replaced by one of the developers in the room. This goes on for an hour or so. This allows everyone to take a turn at showing how they solve the coding problem in baby steps.

---

*. You can read more about coding dojos at http://codingdojo.org/.
†. You can find some examples at http://codekata.com/.

Time to Learn How to Write Tests

Once they're convinced about making the move to TDD, the team members need to learn how to do it. It will give them a boost if someone can work with them who has experience in automated testing and TDD (maybe that's you).

Point them in the direction of commercial training courses to give them a head start. However, if there's no budget for training (or no training courses available in the programming language they're using), the team needs to teach themselves how to write automated tests. Help them set up a regular coding dojo to improve their test-writing skills (see the sidebar on the current page).

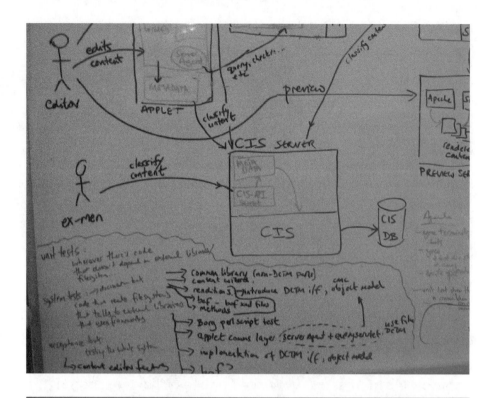

Figure 10.1: WHITEBOARD PICTURE FROM TEST STRATEGY DISCUSSION

Expect the team members to slow down as they come to grips with writing automated tests. When they're making plans, remind the team to allow time for learning to write automated tests. The team should also let their customer know up front that the team velocity is likely to dip while they're in this learning period.

Determining Where to Start Writing Tests

The team won't be able to retrofit tests to existing code in one fell swoop. They'll need to do this iteratively. Help them work out where to start.

Agree on a test strategy with the team.

Gather the team together to agree on a test strategy for how different areas of the code will be tested. Make a sketch of the software architecture on a whiteboard (like the one shown in Figure 10.1). Work through the architecture with the team to determine which parts will benefit most from automated tests. Take a digital

Unit Test Rules by Michael Feathers, Object Mentor

I've used these rules with a large number of teams. They encourage good design and rapid feedback, and they seem to help teams avoid a lot of trouble.

A test is not a unit test if

- it talks to the database,
- it communicates across the network,
- it touches the file system,
- it can't run correctly at the same time as any of your other unit tests, or
- you have to do special things to your environment (such as editing config files) to run it.

Tests that do these things aren't bad. Often they are worth writing, and they can be written in a unit test harness. However, it is important to be able to separate them from true unit tests so that we can keep a set of tests that we can run fast whenever we make our changes.

photo of the whiteboard to document the discussion; revisit this at a later date when the team is ready to look at where to add tests next.

A good place to start is with *unit tests*, as defined in the sidebar on the current page. Code in the middle is usually easy to isolate, so the team should be able to create fast-running unit tests. However, the team is likely to find that any code without automated tests has tangled dependencies. A developer must find a way to isolate the code they are working on, before they can wrap unit tests around it. They'll find some useful techniques for doing this in *Working Effectively with Legacy Code* [Fea04].

Most teams we work with start with a basic rule: they'll write tests for new code and any changes to existing code. Discuss this approach with the team, and check that they're happy to commit to doing this. If following this rule is too overwhelming, work with them to agree on a target of writing a few tests every day so that some minimal progress is made. Make it clear to the team these tests will be most useful if they cover paths through the code that might fail rather than trivial methods. They'll be missing the point if they hit the target by writing tests for getters and setters.

After the team decides where in the codebase they will start adding automated tests, remind them to agree on how they will organize their tests. They'll need to consider whether tests will be stored in the same subdirectories as the code or separately. Adopting a consistent approach to naming tests also helps. And last but not least, everyone on the team needs to be able to run the whole suite of automated tests!

10.2 Continuous Integration

You may find the developers are used to working separately, checking code in every few days. They defer integrating their code because it's time-consuming, but while they put off integrating, the rest of the codebase can change; the longer between integrations, the harder it is.

Continuous Integration (CI) is integrating code changes early and often. Each integration is small, so each should be trivial to integrate. Working this way, the latest code is available to the whole team in small slices, as soon as it's ready, rather than in one big lump. CI connects with doing TDD because tests should pass for the whole integrated codebase, not just on a developer's computer. So, CI is not just integrating code frequently; all tests should pass all of the time too.

As James Shore puts it:[2]

Contrary to popular belief, continuous integration is an attitude, not a tool. It's a shared agreement by the team that:

1. *When we get the latest code from the repository, it will always build successfully and pass all tests.*

2. *We will check in our code every two to four hours.*

We like this quote because the vital part of adopting CI is that the team wholeheartedly embraces this philosophy, making sure all tests pass all the time. When teams try to use CI tools without developing this attitude, developers often don't take responsibility for fixing the build when it breaks.

---

2. http://jamesshore.com/Blog/Continuous-Integration-is-an-Attitude.html

Figure 10.2: BUILD TOKEN

When introducing CI to the team, suggest that they start by following a synchronous CI process. Every time a developer checks in code, they run the build and wait to see whether all tests pass before moving on to develop more code. If the tests don't pass, then the developer needs to fix the problem.

Start by building CI discipline.

For this to work, developers need to avoid treading on one another's toes by attempting to integrate changes at the same time. Lots of teams use a *build token*, which can be any object that makes it obvious to the rest of the team that there's an integration in progress. Teams have a bit of fun with this, which helps establish the CI process as a team ritual. We've seen teams use a rubber chicken, a moo cow, funny hats, and even a "Sword of Integration"[3] made from index cards, in Figure 10.2.

---

3. Demonstrated at XPDay 2008 by Gwyn Morfey, New Bamboo.

Rachel Says...

Don't Force Toys on the Team

Team rituals spring up naturally from the team and evolve over time. Don't be tempted to shortcut this and inflict fun on the team by going out to buy a cute build token yourself. Having toys around the workplace makes it easier for the team to destress and incorporate them into team work, but take care to be sensitive to the company culture. If the team is seen by management to be too frivolous, it can backfire on the team.

Some teams also add a sound to celebrate a successful integration, such as a gong or sound of applause. This acts as a signal for the rest of the team to pull in the changes just checked in.

Although this synchronous CI process sounds more time-consuming than having software detect check-ins and run tests automatically, doing this the long way helps developers learn to take responsibility for fixing broken builds. Once everyone on the team is integrating their code at least a couple of times a day and the build doesn't stay broken, it's time to move to a more asynchronous, software-assisted solution. Keep your eyes open to see whether the team still takes responsibility for fixing broken builds. The key is improving feedback on build status so the team knows as soon as possible that the build is broken.

Improving Feedback on Build Status

If the team makes the move to using a CI server to run the build and let them know the test results, they won't need a build token anymore. Developers just check their code in and move on. Now it becomes important that everyone on the team is alerted when the build is broken because their last check-in could have caused the tests to fail. Email notifications aren't usually the best way to let developers know that the tests are failing because they are likely to have their mail client closed when programming. Instead, try to make the failing tests more visible to the whole team by making the build page more interesting, as Ivan tells

---

Enhancing the Build Page by Ivan Moore, Team Optimization

We used South Park Studio* to create character pictures of everyone on the team to use on our team board. We put these next to stories to show who was working on which story. They were a big hit with the team.

We had been having a problem of builds remaining broken without anyone taking responsibility to fix the build. I adapted our CI tool, Build-o-matic,[†] to scrape the commit messages to find developers' names or initials, match them to these images, and put them in the build results page displayed on our build status monitor.

The effect of having the images in the build page took me by surprise. When people first saw the page, they laughed, and it certainly got everyone's attention. People started taking more notice of the build. Also, when the build was broken, it was fixed more quickly, because it was more directly visible which commit broke the build.

The pictures show who checked in as soon as a modification is detected and the build is started. This meant that people who had just checked in code could easily tell whether the build with their changes was running.

---

*. http://www.sp-studio.de/
†. http://build-o-matic.sourceforge.net/

---

us in the sidebar on the current page. We've also included a snapshot of a build page; see Figure 10.3, on the following page.

Feedback needs to be fast as well as visible. If it takes a long while to run all the tests, more developers may have checked in by the time it finishes. Typically no one jumps to fix it because everyone is sure that it was someone else who broke the build.

10.3 Sustaining Test-Driven Development

So far, we've been talking about how to introduce TDD and CI. However, once the team has installed these practices, you still need to support the team in sustaining these approaches. If the team is already confident in applying TDD, is there anything you can do to help them improve?

Started (Wed Nov 1 12:44:41 2006) took (7 mins 45 secs)
Successful 9064 (Bob + Fred : restored missing validation to fix build)

Started (Wed Nov 1 12:38:14 2006) took (0 mins 42 secs)
Failed 9063 (Josh: completely breaking the build)

Started (Wed Nov 1 12:29:02 2006) took (8 mins 6 secs)
Successful 9062 (Ron and Jim: renamed and refactored repository classes
Noel & Ian: implemented self-awareness feature

Figure 10.3: BUILD PAGE SHOWING AVATARS

Watch out for slow-running tests. The following story shows how a team that was very proud of their tests was held back by slow-running tests. Encourage the team to factor in time to improve their build scripts and infrastructure to avoid this.

Impact of Slow-Running Tests
by Liz

I worked with a team that had a very comprehensive suite of automated acceptance tests; however, the full suite of tests took two hours to run. This meant that a developer couldn't run all of the tests before they checked their work in, so frequently the developers checked in code that broke the tests. By the time they noticed it two hours later, several other developers had also checked in code, and each of them assumed it was the other who had broken the test suite. Consequently, the tests were always failing.

Liz Says...

Ten-Minute Build

The team needs an automated test suite that is quick to run. Otherwise, when tests take a long time to run, developers don't wait for the tests to pass. Pay attention to the time it takes to build the application and run the tests. Whenever this time exceeds the ten-minute threshold, the team needs to invest time into making the tests run faster.

The team did not consider that making sure the acceptance tests passed was part of a user story being completed or part of their definition of "done." Gradually over time, the quality of the codebase got worse and worse, as more and more tests started to fail. The acceptance tests were not adding any value because they weren't passing.

As a coach, I encouraged the developers to speed up the test suite and to stop adding more code when the acceptance tests were failing. However, the project pressure was so great that the developers felt that they needed to concentrate on getting more stories implemented.

One day it was so bad that something had to be done. Some developers worked on fixing the broken tests, while the rest of the team helped the QA team with testing the product. No one would add any more new features until the existing tests passed.

The tests were fixed that day. However, the test suite still ran slowly, so the next day the tests failed again. And they stayed broken for the remainder of the project. More and more corners were cut in an attempt to make the date. As the deadline drew near, no one knew how far off "done" the team was. Eventually they did release, after going through the dreaded testing phase that the automated tests had been written to avoid.

If slow tests are in the minority, the team may be able to isolate long-running tests into a separate test suite that is run in the background. However, if there are a lot of slow-running tests, this can be down to poorly designed tests with too many dependencies on external resources. Maybe the team needs to write more tests that make use of test doubles, such as mock objects or stubs, to fake out these external resources. Another solution is to break the test run over a build farm.

The team may need a lot of support and encouragement to really drive development with tests. Watch out for developers claiming "It's just a one-line change" as a justification for not writing tests. Too many of these one-line changes without tests can turn into an excuse not to write any tests for legacy code.

Work with them to make test coverage more visible. This should be increasing at roughly the same rate as the code grows. Code coverage analysis tools can be used to measure this. Don't forget these tools check only that the tests exercise all the code; they don't test how good those tests are. Be vigilant that coverage is not being fudged with poor tests.

Making Passing Tests Visible
by Liz

I worked with a team that was new to TDD. I posted the number of passing tests and failing tests visibly on the team board. We reviewed the numbers at our daily standup to see how well the team was doing. This helped them keep the tests in mind.

I did this only for a month or so until the team got better at TDD and remembering to make sure all tests were passing.

So, what's left to do if the team has good test coverage and fast-running tests? It's probably time to revisit the test strategy. Encourage them to broaden their horizons to look for new areas of their architecture that they don't have tests for.

10.4 Hurdles

The following are some hurdles you may encounter.

No Test Tools Available

Open source unit-testing frameworks are available for common programming languages. However, some teams have to write code in proprietary programming languages because they're working with third-party software that has its own language or because their company has developed a specialized language of its own and already has a lot of code written in it. If the team finds that there's no commercial or open source tools for writing automated tests in a programming language that they use, this doesn't need to stop them from making the move to automate tests. It is usually possible to write a simple automated test framework—encourage them to consider rolling their own test tools.

Maintain Test-First Discipline

It can be hard to make the shift to a test-first approach when adopting TDD. Expect to find some developers still working in a test-after way. This is natural. For instance, as a developer I may sketch out the code to visualize where to test it; at that point, it's all too easy to slip into writing the solution before the tests. Working in pairs to discuss design can help developers get started with TDD.

If a developer on the team strongly objects to writing tests first but is willing to write automated tests, suggest the team allows this for a trial period. As long as her automated tests achieve a similar level of test coverage as the rest of the team, working test-after may be OK. Watch out for whether this way of working causes problems for other team members, and bring this up at the retrospective.

Everyone Works in Their Own Branch

There are many different branching strategies, but one that is incompatible with Continuous Integration is everyone working in their own branch. Some teams work this way so that developers don't disturb each other while they are working.

This causes a problem because each integration may be quite time-consuming, often revealing misunderstandings within the team caused by developers working in isolation. Each integration also brings with it the risk of breaking other code and introducing defects. The whole point of CI is that small, frequent integrations are quick and painless and that sticking to CI keeps developers aligned.

If you find that the team is deferring integration, we recommend you discuss the problems it can cause with the team. Encourage them to try CI for a couple of weeks and review at the team retrospective.

10.5 Checklist

- Allow plenty of time for making the transition to Test-Driven Development. This is a large change for a team to take on board in one go. Take an iterative approach to introducing TDD. Spend time with the team understanding what the blockers are, and then apply the PrOpER cycle.

- A completely greenfield project can start with writing tests first. When the team has to retrofit tests to existing code, they'll need time to figure out where to start. They can start writing a few automated tests per day or work test-after rather than test-first until they have a handle on how to test any legacy code.

- The whole team has to agree to the approach; all developers will need to write and run tests for TDD to work. Make sure the team understands the problems that TDD will solve.

- Factor time into plans for the team to learn how to write automated tests. Support the team's learning by organizing training and coding dojos.

- Get the team together to agree on a test strategy; unit tests in the middle layer are usually a safe place to start. Don't forget to get agreement on automated testing basics, such as where tests will be stored and how they will be run. Review the test strategy with the team to work out where to go next.

- Continuous Integration is an attitude, not a set of tools. Suggest that the team start with a synchronous CI process before relying on a build server.

- If the team uses a CI server, make it easy for the team to take responsibility for fixing broken tests. Work on making build status visible to the whole team rather than buried in email.

- Watch out for slow-running tests. Encourage the team to factor time into their plans for improving their build scripts and infrastructure. Test coverage can help the team get a better understanding of how well they're doing.

Chapter 11

Clean Code

Keeping your house tidy and clean is obviously important; otherwise, over time it becomes impossible to live in. In the same way, if the team doesn't take time to keep their code clean, it becomes messy and fragile, which slows them down. As their coach, you're there to support them in learning how to keep code clean, tested, and integrated all the time.

Let's take a look at how you can make clean code a focus for the team and get them started with Agile practices such as incremental design, collective code ownership, and pair programming. We'll also share some tips on how to surface and resolve problems that block the team from collaborating to create clean code.

11.1 Incremental Design

Incremental design is simply taking time to improve the design of the software in small steps as you go. Design improvement becomes part of every developer's day. It's done on every user story and is not something left until later. Working this way, developers think about the design of the software as they write tests, as they implement the code to pass those tests, and before they check in their code.

However, making the shift from design up front to incremental design can be a challenge. Help the team strike the right balance between spending time on software design vs. time implementing code to satisfy more user stories.

Breaking Out of Analysis Paralysis

Teams often get stuck in *analysis paralysis* near the start of a project. Help them break out of spending too much time thinking about design without producing working software.

Try to pinpoint what's stopping them from moving forward. Are they trying to work out the correct design for all future requirements? Are they afraid that decisions made now can't be reversed later? Remind them that they don't have a crystal ball to predict all the new requirements that will come up during the project. Further discussion is unlikely to reveal the correct answer, whereas they can prove their ideas by implementing them.

Encourage the team to design for *now* and to keep their design as simple as they can for current needs. We're not saying they have to be deliberately shortsighted—the team can bear in mind the upcoming user stories when making design decisions. Remind developers that rework often improves design. Each time the design is reworked, it is refined and becomes more malleable.

Agreeing On a Way Forward

Disagreements on the team about architectural aspects of the design can also prevent the team from moving forward. These conflicts often bubble up when there's a power struggle between developers with different expertise in the team. A common debate is how much logic to put in front end, middleware, or stored procedures. The team gets stuck because they don't know how to resolve the disagreement by themselves.

If the team reaches an impasse, run a team workshop to evaluate the pros and cons of different design options. Where possible, bring an expert, from outside the team, to the workshop to provide an independent perspective. Make sure each alternative gets equal airtime and consideration. Suggest the team write up each design on a whiteboard. This helps move the debate away from the personalities and onto the issues. Encourage the team to pick one design to follow for the next iteration and agree to review concerns in their next retrospective. Suggest this choice be made by an anonymous ballot if you're concerned about the pressure within the team.

Making Time for Design

Far more often than analysis paralysis, we find teams suffer from the opposite problem: not spending enough time on design. Developers can be tempted to skimp on design because software design is invisible from the outside, so the customer can't see it. When they're under pressure to deliver, developers often slide into just writing code that works without cleaning up the design; skimping on the design enables them to deliver user stories faster in the short-term. But without attention to design, the code becomes hard to understand and difficult to change, which eventually slows the whole team down and in serious cases can lead to a whole codebase being thrown away.

Help the team keep design in mind as they implement the user stories. Remind them when they're planning to allow time in their estimates for design discussions and refactoring. This cannot be done by adding a design task to every story—design is not a separate task that can be checked off as complete. Design needs to become an integrated part of how the team develops all code. Where some stories require further design discussion, add a card on the team board as a reminder to have this conversation.

You can also help the team keep clean code in mind by working with them to incorporate a design review into their definition of "done." They can make a team agreement that another developer must eyeball code before it's checked in to ensure that the code (and unit tests) can be easily understood by at least one other team member. Or they can choose to implement this by pair programming so all production code is written by two developers working as a pair.

Get a whiteboard that the team can gather around for informal design discussions. Make sure this is close to where the developers sit, rather than in a meeting room, because design conversations are often spontaneous. When a developer wants to explain something, he can just grab a marker and draw a sketch to help illustrate his point. Help the team get started using their new whiteboard by using it in design discussions yourself.

When the team members follow an incremental design approach, they pay attention to the design of the code throughout the development of each story. They talk about design before they implement the code, and they clean up the design as they go. However, it helps to make design changes in small steps rather than changing too many things at once. Encourage the team to use refactoring to make one small change at a time rather than make sweeping changes all in one go.

Refactoring

Refactoring is the activity of improving software design without changing its behavior. It's done in baby steps by applying one small improvement at a time, such as *Rename Field* or *Extract Method*. After each

Explaining Refactoring to Your Customer

A team may never need to explain what refactoring is to their customer, if they manage to keep applying small refactorings as part of each story. However, developers often mention opportunities for refactoring at the daily standup, and task cards for refactorings may appear on the team board. This is bound to make your customer curious, and if refactoring is explained as design improvement, it sounds like an optional "nice to have" activity.

We find that it helps to explain it by analogy. Refactoring is like tidying up at home. If every time I come back from shopping or from a business trip, I sling down my things and don't put them away, pretty soon my house is a mess. I can't find anything. I may end up buying new items because I can't find the ones I know I already have. It becomes more difficult to move around the house—there are piles of stuff everywhere! I may even break something because it's obscured by other stuff on top of it.

Refactoring is the necessary act of putting code in the right place, where other developers can find it quickly and easily. It's keeping code organized and decluttered. Developers need to do refactoring, or they can end up with the same code in several places, which takes more effort to maintain. Refactoring is not the aesthetic organization of the code, such as applying feng shui to your home—it's basic housekeeping.

refactoring, the tests should be run to see that they still pass and if so, it should be possible to check in the code. Our favorite guide to refactoring is Bill Wake's *Refactoring Workbook* [Wak04] because it includes exercises that you can run through with the team.

Refactoring the code makes it easier to maintain in two ways:

Improving readability by restructuring and renaming code

Reducing redundant code by consolidating and deleting unused code

Readable Code

The team needs to write code that is easy to understand by anyone else on the team and is also self-explanatory to those maintaining the code in years to come. As Kent Beck says in *Implementation Patterns* [Bec07], "There's no magic to writing code other people can read. It's like all writing—know your audience, have a clear overall structure in mind, express the details so they contribute to the story."

Beck goes on to explain the essential step to communicating through code is making a conscious choice to care about the needs of other people. Help developers on the team see how important it is to write for someone else reading the code. Practicing collective code ownership helps with this by exposing every team member to code they didn't write. As they complain about the way someone else wrote the code, they become more aware of the need to write their code more clearly. Pair programming goes a step further by exposing them directly to each other's programming styles so they get an appreciation of the thinking behind the code and a chance to intervene and teach their teammates better ways to express themselves.

We recommend you take some time to look through the code to get a sense of how the team is doing with software design. This may reveal areas where the team needs further coaching, such as poor design or misconceptions about requirements. You may even find comments in the code that give you a clue that there are disagreements about the design and that help you surface issues that have not been resolved within the team.

Telltale Comments
by Rachel

I have noticed that developer gripes are sometimes revealed in comments, and these can provide some useful insights. Here's an example from a project I worked on:

```
/* Ideally this would be done as part of a lazy load implementation on the reference
get method in each of the business objects. It would then use the DAO to find the
objects it owns, effectively implementing a manual version of container managed
relations (CMR) in the Entity EJB world. However, this is impossible thanks to our
unconventional method of holding the database connection and passing from the
top session layer down to the DAOs. Consequently, the only method of producing a
complete tract object with all its children is to manually build the object here. Very
nasty, completely against the idea of the DAO design pattern and the service layer
separation, and very bad for maintenance.*/
```

This comment told me that there was at least one developer on the team who cared about the integrity of the design but felt like they were fighting a losing battle. I started to work with this developer to justify the much-needed refactoring of the tangled dependencies to his manager on the basis that this was a barrier to unit testing.

Liz Says...

__No Comments__

Encourage the team to avoid writing comments; they clutter the code and can't be relied on to be accurate. Good code is clear and obvious without comments. If you see a lot of comments in the code or overhear developers explaining the code, this suggests that some refactoring is needed.

Refactoring Tools

Tools can also help the team stick with incremental design by making design improvement easier to do. Having automated support for common refactorings (provided by such tools as ReSharper for C# or Eclipse for Java) makes it quicker and less error prone to make changes to design. Coach the team to take time to get their development environment working well.

Simply having refactoring tools installed is not enough; developers also need to know how and when to use them. If some team members already know how to use the tools, pair programming can be a great way to transfer the knowledge. If everyone is new to refactoring, set some time aside in the plan for team learning. You could encourage the team to run a coding dojo (see the sidebar on page 141) to get them talking about the design of their code and tests.

11.2 Collective Code Ownership

Talk to the team about trying *collective code ownership*, where any team member can edit any piece of code. Now any developer can start working on the next story without waiting for the person who wrote the code to be available.

Team collaboration plays a big part in collective code ownership. Without some degree of collaboration, developers can be working at cross-purposes without realizing it. Notice the level of conversation amongst developers on the team. If they don't talk to each other, this is a clue that their work may be disconnected. Battles could be playing out in the code without being discussed; each developer rewrites the code to suit their own taste, and the result is like a patchwork quilt that's full of holes. Your challenge is to get the "team" to join forces and work as a real team rather than suffering in silence.

Coding Style

Collective code ownership is easier when the team follows a consistent approach to design and coding style. We're not saying that they need to create a formal coding standards document. They simply need to establish a "house style" that everyone agrees to follow.

Bring the whole team together to work out what coding style they want to adopt. This can be a tough debate to manage. There's no correct answer about what style is best, and developers often have strong preferences

> Bring the whole team together to agree on a coding style.

about code layout based on how they learned to program. Still, it's worth pushing for because once the team has a consistent style, their code is more readable, and less time is wasted on reformatting code to personal taste. You can use gradients of agreement (Section 2.4, *Building Agreement*, on page 27) to determine when you have enough consensus to be able to follow each proposed guideline. Or even simpler, take a thumb vote like the team in our story.

Team Agrees to Some Coding Guidelines

The team is gathered in the workspace around their new whiteboard. Joe stands up and clears his throat. "OK, I've called this meeting so we can make a start on cleaning up our code."

He walks over to the whiteboard and picks up a marker pen. "Let's get started with some style guidelines that we can all agree to follow."

Damian rolls his eyes. "Don't we have better things to do than talk about where we put curly brackets?"

Joe reminds the team, "We talked about cleaning the code up in our last retrospective. We've got to act together on this, or the new code will get as bad as PLib."

Joe looks around at the team expectantly. "Does anyone have a guideline that you think makes sense for us all to follow?"

Larry gazes out of the window; there are dark shadows under his eyes. Joe calls over to him, "Larry, are you still with us?"

Larry slowly refocuses. "Sure, I'd like us to make up our minds on naming tests. Some start with Test, and others end with Test—that seems pretty random to me. Personally, I don't have a preference, but it would make tests easier to find if we could stick to one or the other."

Damian looks surprised. "Right! That makes sense to me."

"Any objections?" asks Joe as he writes up on the board *Henceforth, we shall name our test classes Testxxx, not xxxTest.* "OK, let's have a thumb vote."

Damian says, "That's a no-brainer!" holding up his thumb.

Larry and Joe hold up their thumbs too. Damian looks over at Rebecca, "Are you OK with that too?" She nods, holding up her thumb.

Then she blurts out, "What about a guideline for keeping all of our functions really short? That would help us make sure each function does only one thing. You know, like Bob Martin says in his *Clean Code* [Mar08] book."

Damian leans back in his chair sucking his pen. "That's sounds good, but I'd vote with sideways thumb until I know what you mean by short."

Rebecca ponders for a moment and then says, "In college, we were told a function should not take more space than I can see on the screen. But we have big monitors. I think we need to go smaller than that so each function does only one thing."

Joe picks up the marker again. "Maybe we can narrow it down to a number of lines of code?"

Rebecca scratches her chin and then suggests, "What about saying all our functions should be no more than ten lines long?"

Damian frowns. "I'm not so sure. Remember, we've got some old PLib code with some pretty long functions."

Larry nods. "Some of them are more than 200 lines long, and it's really hard to tell what they do without printing them out because they don't fit on the screen."

"I've got a proposal for you," says Joe as writes the following on the board: *Any NEW functions should be less than ten lines long.* "Does that sound OK?" Everyone raises their thumbs.

Damian leans forward. "We could even measure that using our static analysis toolkit. Then we could see whether these coding standards are making a difference. If we're following them, then the number of long functions should start falling week by week, and we could graph that."

"Would you be on for setting that up?" ask Joe.

Damian grabs an index card and writes out a task to go on the team board. "Sure! I've been meaning to do some digging around to see what we can use it for. Maybe we can even get it hooked into our CI build."

"I volunteer to print out the stats to put on our team board until you get the CI build working," adds Rebecca.

Once the team has their new coding guidelines, encourage them to discuss whether it's important to measure how well they're doing against any benchmarks that they've chosen.

In our example, the team is planning to run a static analysis tool to measure how many functions have more than ten lines of code. Watch out, though—generating too much data can just create noise. Help the team get clear on what they will do with this new information. They can plot the results on a chart and either pin this to the team board or update it dynamically on a build monitor screen.

Keeping the results visible will remind everyone of the agreement and also show whether they're keeping it. After a few weeks or months, the team should find they've improved and no longer need to chart how many long functions there are. However, if the trend isn't running as expected, the team needs to understand why. Their retrospective is a good time to discuss this.

Working with Specialists

Although getting team agreement on coding style may feel like the hardest part of adopting collective code ownership, it's actually much harder to get developers on the team to stop specializing by picking bits of the codebase that they consider as their own. It is quicker for someone who has worked on a module before to fix any bugs in it and be the person to add more related features, but doing this can create scheduling bottlenecks.

Specializing also makes it less necessary for the team to talk to each other about design and ask for help when they're stuck. You'll notice the developers don't talk to each other much if they're specializing in this way. Pair programming can help prevent this. Some teams we work with follow a simple rule that one person from each pair must swap out every day. This encourages everyone on the team to move between the user stories rather than sticking with the same story.

Rachel Says...

Permission to Care About Code

Most software developers love to write code, but many are fed up with the crufty state of the existing codebase they're working on. Try to rekindle their personal passion for code so they can rebuild a sense of pride in their work. They can enjoy coding again, so what's stopping them?

Self-censorship may be part of the problem. A developer may assume they will not be allowed time to improve things so they don't even explain what they think needs to be done in order to do the job properly. They keep putting the short-term needs of the business ahead of their own professional judgment.

They may be worried that their opinion won't be respected and that it will be difficult to quantify the benefits. Getting the team together, in planning, to discuss the tasks and estimates makes this a team decision, not a personal one. If they join forces to work together rather than battle on by themselves, they may be able to make a difference.

Fixing Broken Windows

You'll also need to watch out that collective code ownership does not degrade into developers abstaining responsibility for the code. In *The Pragmatic Programmer* [HT00], Andy Hunt and Dave Thomas talk about the "broken windows" theory. Small signs of not caring about the code can lead to bigger transgressions.

Try applying the PrOpER coaching cycle we talked about (see Section 1.4, *How to Start Coaching*, on page 11). Talk to the developers about what's bothering them the most about the code. You may need to talk to them individually to get to the bottom of their concerns. There may be a particular area of the code that is really bad or a conflict within the team about a design issue. Or, where the team is working on an old messy codebase, they may simply be overwhelmed by the task of cleaning it up. Help them form a plan of action to renovate the code. Simply recognizing the problem and breaking it down into bite-size pieces can make a big difference and help reengage developers who had given up.

11.3 Pair Programming

Pair programming is two people working together—at the same computer, solving the same problem. Each person plays an active role in creating the software; the person actively typing is known as the *driver*, and her partner is the *navigator* who looks ahead to consider next steps and potential pitfalls. Pairs swap fluidly between these roles.

If you're trying to persuade the team to try pair programming, here are some benefits that pair programming generates over time:

- Code is higher in quality, because it is constantly being reviewed.
- Good practice is shared more widely amongst the team.
- Developers are interrupted less, because people tend not to interrupt people working together.
- More than one developer knows each part of the code.
- A uniform coding style is implemented, which makes it easy for everyone to work together.
- Team bonding improves, because the team learns from each other and enjoys working together.

If you know how to program, it's often tempting to make suggestions about how developers should write the code. Be careful, because you may be wasting your time—developers are likely to ignore your coding experience if you're not programming on the project. They may also think that you're overstepping your role and interfering in how they do their job, so give such advice sparingly. However, pair programming can be a great way to coach individual developers. Here are some tips to improve your own style if you haven't tried it for coaching before.

When you're driving, don't just type code in silence. Demonstrate that an important aspect of pair programming is explaining what you're doing and why. When your pair has the keyboard, make sure you don't become a backseat driver. There's nothing more unnerving than pairing with someone who jumps on every typo and shouts out keyboard shortcuts all the time.

> **Explain what you're doing and why.**

Stay open to suggestions from your pair, even if they are a novice programmer. There's a phenomenon called the *beginner's mind*: someone with fresh eyes may see more options than you. So even if you see a very obvious solution, be willing to try out the solution that your pair suggests. If it fails, then they will have learned something, and if it succeeds, then you learn something! Read more about how Arlo Belshee's

Liz Says...
Two Monitors

Two people sharing one computer can feel uncomfortable. To ease this, plug two monitors, two keyboards, and two mice into the same PC (as in this photograph). Make both monitors display the same code. This allows people to pair without invading each other's personal space. It also makes it easy to swap between driver and navigator roles.

team experimented with pair-swap times to leverage this in his paper "Promiscuous Pairing and Beginner's Mind" published in *Proceedings of the Agile 2005 Conference* [Bel05].

We sometimes see pair programming done badly, where one person is doing all the work and the other is just watching them type. You should see interaction between pairs. Effective pairing is a dynamic dance, with the keyboard frequently and spontaneously shifting between the two. There's a video clip on YouTube, *Real Programmers Use Sign Language*, that shows two developers gesturing a lot while pairing.[1]

---

1. http://pairing.www.youtube.com/watch?v=nqYqQUfPCp8

You can also get a sense of pair programming interactions by watching online broadcasts of pairing sessions.[2]

Normally, one person shouldn't have the keyboard for more than ten minutes at a time. Introduce ping-pong programming (see the sidebar on the following page) to help the team get used to swapping control within a pair.

At first, pair programming can be frustrating for developers; often it means slowing down to help their teammates rather than getting on with producing code. You'll notice, over time, that the team gets to know each other's foibles, and as they do so, they can focus more on the task at hand without distractions over style, producing code that is far more readable.

Remember that pair programming is very intense; it requires a huge amount of concentration. Remind the team that it's a good idea to take a break every hour or so. Some teams use a kitchen timer for this, or they use the pomodoro technique to encourage pairs to take breaks, as described in the sidebar on page 167.

Also encourage developers to swap between pairs. The daily standup is an ideal time for the team to talk about whether they're going to pair up on any tasks—and if so, who with. Suggest that the team create a pairing ladder (see Section 8.2, *Big Visible Charts*, on page 113) so they can see whether team members are pairing with each other evenly.

11.4 Hurdles

The following are some hurdles you may encounter.

A Developer Doesn't Like Pair Programming

Often, we find that some developers on a team enjoy pair programming, while others do not. Look out for signs of resistance to pair programming, and try to understand what's causing it.

A common reason is that some developers don't know how to pair properly. If one person is merely watching while the other person does all the work, it is not surprising that they don't enjoy it. Explain how pair programming interaction should work, and encourage them to try ping-pong programming.

---

2. http://pairwith.us/

Ping-Pong Programming

Ping-pong programming is an approach to pair programming that ensures both members of the pair take a turn at the keyboard.*

- The first developer writes a failing test and then passes the keyboard to his pair.
- The second developer writes just enough code to make the test pass.
- They then work together to refactor the code that has just been written.
- Then the cycle can start again with the second person writing a new failing test and handing the keyboard back to the first person.

---

*. http://c2.com/cgi/wiki?PairProgrammingPingPongPattern

Discuss with the team how much pair programming they feel is necessary. When do they feel it is appropriate—when is it expected, and when is it optional? Do they want a working agreement about this? Some teams choose to pair on all production code, and other teams pair only on difficult problems. If developers won't pair, then their code should at least get some code review.

A Developer Doesn't Follow Team Coding Practices

You cannot force a developer to care about code quality. However, it's important as a coach to care when a team member doesn't follow team agreements. For example, a developer might regularly check in code that doesn't compile before she goes home, leaving her teammates to fix the problems.

If disrespect for team agreements bothers the team, then start by talking with the developer to understand why. It may be that she's forgotten the team agreement or not understood how it applies to her work. If she's aware and going against the agreement deliberately, this could signal that she might be better suited to working on another team.

Although the whole team could talk with her about it in their retrospective, we recommend you avoid that situation because it can easily turn into scapegoating.

Pomodoro Technique

The *pomodoro* technique* is a time-management technique to help improve focus and concentration created by Francesco Cirillo at XPLabs.

Work in timeboxes of twenty-five minutes, followed by a five-minute break. After four timeboxes, take a longer break. Each of these timeboxes is called a *pomodoro*, Italian for "tomato," because of the tomato-shaped kitchen timer that was originally used.

At the start of the pomodoro, turn off your email, your instant messaging client, and your phone. Set the timer to twenty-five minutes, and then work. Do nothing else. If someone interrupts you, tell them you'll get back to them after this pomodoro. If your mind wanders, note down the thought, and get back to what you're meant to be doing.

When the timer rings, take a break. Mark a tick on the story card, or personal journal, and rest for a few minutes.

At the beginning of the day, make a plan with the team for how to use your pomodoro timeboxes. At the end of the day, record all the pomodoro spent on each activity to help improve future estimates.

---

*. http://www.pomodorotechnique.com/

Gaps in Programming Languages Create a Barrier to Pair Programming

Your team may be working on a layered system where the front, middle, and back-end technologies are very different. The developers on the team may find the learning curve too steep to switch from programming in one layer to another. In this situation, pair programming makes sense only between the developers who are familiar with that language. For example, it does not usually make sense to pair a C++ developer with a JavaScript developer.

Pair programming is not a substitute for training. If a developer on the team needs to learn C++ or some other language, they may be better off taking a training course or reading a book than pair programming. Also watch out for developers who are concerned about diluting their specialist knowledge.

11.5 Checklist

- Help the team strike a balance between spending time on software design vs. time implementing code. The team needs to focus on designing for the user stories they know about rather than second-guessing the customer.

- Remind the team during the planning process to allow time for incremental design. Get into the habit of using a whiteboard in the team workspace for design discussions.

- Encourage the team to improve software design gradually by refactoring before every check-in rather than building up technical debt. Refactoring tools lower the barrier to making design improvements. Make sure the team knows how to use them.

- Bring the whole team together to agree on a common coding style. If the team doesn't adopt pair programming, recommend they incorporate peer code reviews into their definition of "done."

- Help the team formulate a plan to renovate any areas of the code where design has decayed. Fixing broken windows helps the team keep the standard of design up.

- Use pair programming to get two heads on difficult problems and spread knowledge within the team. Set the team workspace up so that pair programming is comfortable, for example, two monitors displaying the same desktop.

- Introduce ping-pong programming to encourage pairs to swap between the roles of driver and navigator. Watch that pairs take enough breaks and swap partners rather than forming pair cliques.

Part IV

Listening to Feedback

Seek customer feedback to improve the software.
  ► Guiding principle

Chapter 12

Demonstrating Results

If you ever had a school project that involved a show-and-tell to the class, you'll know that being asked to demonstrate your work is a strong motivator. It's the same for Agile teams. Having a demo motivates them to get everything done in time.

Surprisingly, many Agile teams treat the *demo* meeting as an optional extra. Here are some reasons we've encountered:

Nothing to show The team hasn't planned for their iteration to result in software that can be demonstrated.

Going live The team makes a live release at the end of the iteration, and a demo seems pointless.

Customer in the team The team shows the software to the customer during the iteration, so they don't see that a demo adds any value.

These factors are good reasons for changing the format of the iteration demo, but in our opinion the answer is not to scrap the iteration demo. The iteration demo builds trust and accountability between the team and the business, so don't be tempted to skip it.

Let's walk through how you can help the team run effective demos that feel useful and productive.

12.1   Preparing for the Demo

Remember, the secret to a successful meeting lies in the preparation. You'll find this is especially true for the iteration demo.

Plan to build demonstrable stories.	The team sows the seeds for a successful demo in iteration planning. Encourage the team to figure out how user stories can be demonstrated to stakeholders. If this is difficult, suggest a compromise that at least one or two user stories can be shown.

Who Attends the Demo

Let everyone on the team know that they're all expected to attend the demo. We often encounter managers who worry this will be a waste of the team's time. Protect the team's right to demonstrate their own work; otherwise, the demo loses its power to motivate them.

Most teams also use the iteration demo as an opportunity to demonstrate what they've built to the wider organization. Suggest that the customer decide which stakeholders to invite to the demo. She could invite representatives from sales and marketing functions or people from other technical teams such as architects, security specialists, and operations. Remind someone on the team to send an invitation out to everyone, a week or so before the demo, so they can block off time for it in their calendars.

It's great if senior executives can come, because this gives the team a chance to show off their work. However, if this person cannot come at the regular demo time, warn the team not to extend their iteration to accommodate this senior stakeholder. Instead, the team can arrange a separate demo session so he can see the latest release.

Brief stakeholders on the iterative process.	Brief any stakeholders who have not been to a demo before—they need to understand the team is following an iterative process and that what they'll see isn't the finished product.

Finalize the Running Order

On the last day of the iteration, the team needs to develop a drill for getting ready to run the demo meeting. Remind the team about this at the daily standup. Here are some things they can do to prepare:

- Clarify which stories are complete and ready to demo.
- Decide on a running order for presenting the stories.
- Agree who will be presenting which stories.
- Organize a run-through to rehearse the demo.

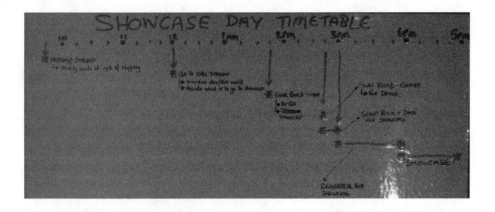

Figure 12.1: TIMETABLE FOR LAST DAY OF ITERATION

Some teams also put a visible timetable up in their workspace to remind them what needs to be done to prepare; see Figure 12.1 (this organization calls the demo a *showcase*).

The following story illustrates the typical conversations that happen on the day of the demo.

Getting Ready to Demo

We join the team as they are partway through their daily standup. Raj, the new project manager, has an announcement for the team: "I couldn't book your usual room for the iteration demo. So, we'll be up on the 11th floor. I'm going up to check out the network connection after this. We just need access to Jupiter over the network, right?"

"If we're in the fancy board room, then network access should be fine. I was in there for a meeting with ops last week, and we had no problem accessing the bug tracker from there." said Damian, who's wearing his favorite *Simpsons* T-shirt. "Who's bringing the donuts this week?"

"It's my turn, but do you mind if we have fruit this week?" Joe grins pointing out a bag of apples and oranges under his desk.

"Great!" chirps Rebecca. "No sugary snacks suits me! I'm in training for a 10K run next month."

"Thanks, Joe," says Raj glancing at his watch. "Now can I just check what we're planning to demo? We've got Mark, the head of sales, coming along this week, so it needs to be slick. So, all the stories on the board in the Done column are ready, except ISBN search, which is still under test. Is that right?" turning to Larry the tester who's looking sleepy and sipping coffee from a *Star Trek* mug.

"Oh yeah, that's ready too. Amanda and I checked the bug fix yesterday, but I forgot to move the story over to Done."

"Great! Sounds like we're all set!" says Raj keen to get on with his day.

"What about working out who's showing what?" adds Joe "I worked on ISBN search, so it makes sense if I do that. Rebecca, are you OK to show the other stories?"

"Yup, I guess so...," says Rebecca hesitantly.

"Don't look so worried. It'll be a piece of cake! And Mark will be blown away when he sees the book carousel!" adds Joe.

"OK, but can I hand over to you if we hit problems accessing the database?" Rebecca says still looking a little worried.

"No worries. Those problems we had last week were down to the server move. It should all be fine this time around. Eh, Damian?" and Damian nods in agreement.

At that moment, Amanda appears with a bunch of index cards in her hand "Hey there! I've just come off a teleconference with our Singapore office talking through their ideas for the next set of stories. Did I miss the standup? "

"Yes, I think we're all set for the demo," smiles Raj. "The only story that didn't make it is recommendations engine spike, and that was really a 'stretch story' in case we finished early."

"Anything special that we should be aware of from the sales side? Mark hasn't promised any new features to customers without checking that we can implement them, has he?" joked Damian half-seriously.

Amanda paused a moment, and then said, "I think we're fine this week. I'll be really interested to hear what he thinks about the carousel, though."

Rebecca still looks nervous and asks, "Amanda, I'm demonstrating the carousel. Can I walk through how to do that with you before the meeting?"

Amanda smiles. "Sure! But first let me get a coffee."

The daily standup ends with Raj heading off upstairs and Amanda and Rebecca going off to the kitchen.

Look back through this story. You'll see that there's more than one team member who reminds the team what needs to be done to prepare for the demo. This is what you're working toward as an Agile coach. When the team is taking responsibility and getting themselves ready, you can take a backseat rather than being center stage orchestrating the meeting.

Technical Setup

The last thing the team wants is a technical hitch to spoil the demo. Remind them that software that works in a development environment may not work when accessed from a meeting room over the network. Recommend they demonstrate software only from a clean integration environment that has been tested—still check that this can be reached over the network from the meeting room where the demo will be held. Another time-saver is to compile a crib sheet on a wiki page that lists locations of key resources, such as links and filenames, which will be used in the demo.

> **Dying on Stage**
> *by Rachel*
>
> I have seen some disastrous demos. One was in the team workspace, and people at the demo were expected to walk from one developer's desk to the next and to look over the developer's shoulder at software running on their desktop monitor. No one could really see what was being demonstrated properly, there was no running order, and people were expected to stand around doing this for two hours.
>
> Another team held their demo between two remote teams using shared desktops without *any* representation from the customer team! The software demonstrated was a rag-bag of half-complete features that were carried over from past iterations. However, the worst thing was the computer setup for working with the remote team—no one could properly hear what they were saying because of an echo on the line, and yet the team continued with this for more than an hour.

Before the meeting starts, do the following:

- Set up any equipment required for the demo, such as a projector, a conference phone, and marker pens.

- Check network connections.

- Remind the team that the meeting is about to start.

12.2 Everyone Plays a Part

Start the meeting with an introduction from the customer. She gives an overview of the goal of the iteration and the user stories that were chosen for development.

Liz Says. . .

Do Food

Bringing food to a meeting is a good way to relax people and make the meeting friendlier. It is a nice way to break up a long meeting or to encourage people to arrive on time. Some teams take turns bringing biscuits or donuts to meetings.

Now, the spotlight turns on the team. What will they be showcasing today? Before showing the software, it's important for the team lead to let everyone know the running order and also whether there are any important stories that are not ready yet. Encourage them to be clear about any shortfall from the start, because this helps maintain the focus on what is being demonstrated. The team can discuss why a shortfall occurred after demonstrating the software or defer this until their iteration retrospective.

Next, it's the turn of the team to present their work. Some team members may not be keen to take a turn because presenting in front of senior stakeholders can be quite nerve-racking. Encourage each team member to take their share of the limelight in iteration demos, but take care not to force this; instead, make it a team decision who presents in the meeting.

It's great for the team to hear praise for their work, but there are usually some holes spotted too. During the demonstration, ensure that feedback, both positive and negative, is captured. Take notes unobtrusively on index cards rather than writing them up on a whiteboard because this can distract from the demo.

Before the meeting ends, review the main points of feedback with the group to check that none has been missed. Suggestions for enhancements or new features will probably go into the pot to feed future planning sessions. Warn the team not to make any promises about getting these done in the next iteration—that decision won't be made until the next planning session.

Before closing the meeting, take a last opportunity to agree on what team velocity should be recorded. If serious bugs were spotted during the demo, the team may decide not to count the points for that story. If the team significantly underdelivered, they may also need to discuss changes to their release plan before dispersing.

Now, let's see how our fictional team run their demo.

Demonstrating Book Search

It's 10:55, Raj stands up and reminds the team that they need to get going. "Sometimes the elevator can be pretty slow, so let's make our way up to 11th floor."

"I'm taking the stairs! Bet I'll get there first!" chimes Rebecca.

"I'd join you, but I've got this fruit to carry," adds Joe, walking off in the direction of the elevators.

Damian looks as if he's still buried in coding. "Come on, Damian!" calls Rebecca. "The demo is starting in a few minutes!"

Damian locks his screen and follows the others.

The team arrives at the meeting room to find Raj has set up the projector already displaying their team wiki page. They file into the plush board room, and Joe places his bag of shiny green apples on the table. Larry grabs one and flops down in one of the fancy leather chairs. Rebecca perches next to him, looking nervous. Mark and his sales team arrive a few moments later with Amanda.

Amanda kicks off the meeting, "Welcome, everyone. I'm sure we're all looking forward to seeing the latest software. The goal of iteration 4 was to improve book search. Raj, can you pull up the list of stories?"

Raj opens the iteration 4 wiki page, which lists the user stories. All of the stories are marked as "done" except for the last, recommendations engine spike, which is marked as "blocked."

"Shall I give a quick summary of what we did?" ask Joe. Amanda nods.

"Our main focus has been to make it easy for our customers to find the book they're looking for. We've implemented searching for books by ISBN and also a carousel so users can browse books by genre. We also planned to investigate how to implement a recommendation engine, but we're still waiting on the RX team for their new interface. I'll be showing you the ISBN search that I worked on with Damian. Then I'll hand over to Rebecca to walk you through the book carousel."

Joe fires up a web browser, pastes in the URL to the server, and the home page opens. He keys in an ISBN number, and the book page loads.

Mark frowns, "I see the dollar price, but where's the Add to Cart button?"

Amanda steps in, "That was out of scope this iteration. I'll be feeding that into the next iteration."

"Any other questions?" asks Joe. "Over to you, Rebecca," he says, sliding the keyboard across the table to her.

Rebecca selects Travel in the book genre menu. The book carousel opens. She flicks through.

Mark asks, "Does this work in the new Chrome browser?"

Rebecca turns to Larry, "Did you test it against that?"

"Yup. It works just fine."

Mark looks pleased. Then he gets out his new flashy cell phone. "Can you check it also works on this?"

Damian looks up. "We'll discuss stories for mobile devices in our next planning session."

"So...," says Amanda looking around the table. "I think we can declare both of the stories that were demonstrated as "done." We're not counting the recommendations engine spike, so that makes the team velocity 11 points."

Raj grabs the keyboard and enters the new velocity on the iteration 4 wiki page.

After the meeting, make sure that the team creates new user stories for improvements suggested in the demo. There's no need to estimate them yet because these will be taken along to iteration planning.

After a successful demo, encourage the team to celebrate what they've achieved. If the team isn't used to doing this themselves, then get the ball rolling. Buy donuts, or take them out for drinks after work.

Finally, if things didn't go so well in the demo, discuss what went wrong in the retrospective.

12.3 Releasing the Software

You'll find a lot of Agile literature about planning iterative releases but very little on how Agile teams actually release software. Just because the iteration has ended doesn't mean the release must go out. A decision needs to be made about whether the software is ready for release.

The team needs to get together with their customer and check the following items:

- Has the software been tested adequately?

- Are there any showstopper bugs?

- Is this a good time for end users to get a new release?

- Has the relevant documentation been done (such as release notes)?

- Does the team need to nominate a team member to support the release?

- Can the release be rolled back if problems are encountered?

Human intervention may be required to release software, but this can be a source of mistakes. Encourage the team to automate their deployment process as much as they can. If they're pushing their software onto servers managed by other teams, consider creating a suite of *deployment tests* to check whether the deployment environment is "fit for deployment."[1] Deployment tests check that any preconditions that must in place for the software to run, such as specific libraries, directory paths, and database access, are in place *before* the software is deployed. These tests can also help the team pinpoint whether problems encountered after the release goes live are being caused by changes in the environment rather than the software.

12.4 Hurdles

The following are some hurdles you may encounter.

The Software Doesn't Work in the Demo

It's embarrassing when the demo does not go as planned. This is usually a result of poor preparation. Check that the software works in the meeting room before the demo and that the meeting room computer has all the necessary hardware and software.

If this was caused by a developer staging last-minute fixes just before the demo, recommend to the team that they demonstrate a labeled release candidate build rather than the latest build.

---

1. http://www.buildmonkey.com/papers/AgileDeployment.pdf

No Stories Have Been Completed

If the team has arranged a demo and then hits problems that prevent them from having any completed stories to demonstrate, they need to consider canceling the demo. Don't take this decision lightly because doing this sends a signal to the team and to the stakeholders that it's not important to deliver working software at the end of every iteration.

Encourage the team to be open about the situation, and make an offer to show the product as it is. However, they may want to warn any important stakeholders, in case they feel their time has been wasted. The exposure to disappointed stakeholders may galvanize the team to do better next time. Remind the team that they can still get some useful feedback on the software even if it's not quite finished.

Reasons for the shortfall should be discussed in the iteration retrospective. For the next iteration, help the team to slice the stories smaller and then to focus on getting a few stories to "done" rather than many in progress.

Having nothing finished leaves the team with a problem: their velocity is zero. Be aware that if the team demonstrates software that doesn't meet their definition of "done," it gives the impression it's finished and the team is ready to get on with new stories. Make sure the customer understands that there is still work to do before the team can take on more stories. When the team is running significantly behind, suggest that they revise their release plan to make the impact on release dates more visible. If the team delays proper testing until the next iteration, there is a danger that the team will slip into a mini-waterfall and the testers won't catch up.

The decision of what to demo is probably most difficult if the software is nearly working but there are still some open bug reports. Review the bug reports. Are these truly showing serious problems, or are these more in the category of reminders that some inconsistencies have been found? Check with the whole team, including your testers, to see whether they are happy to go ahead and demo a story that has outstanding bugs. If the team wants to go ahead and demo software with bugs, then there is a risk that this may be taken as a signal that it's OK not to fix bugs before the demo. During the iteration, watch to see that developers don't start ignoring feedback from testers. If they do, then this may need to be discussed in the retrospective.

Demo Relies on Software from Other Teams

If the team is building a part of a larger product and is working with other teams, then it may be worth holding a joint demonstration so everyone gets to see the product as a whole. If this is not possible, create software stubs so that the team can demonstrate their software running against these.

Our Software Has No User Interface

It's really hard to get customers interested in a software demo if they can't follow a demo because there's no user interface. Encourage the team to create visualization of data processing to make some sort of demonstration possible. Ultimately, this is an indication that the teams might need to scope the work differently; they may consider moving to developing features from the front end to the back end rather than component-based development.

12.5 Checklist

- Work with the team in planning to ensure user stories that can be demonstrated.

- Make sure the whole team, including the customer, attends the demo. Encourage the customer to invite stakeholders from the wider organization along to the demo. Brief any stakeholders who are new to Agile that what they'll be seeing isn't the final product.

- Remind the team on the last day of the iteration to review what is and is not ready for demo. Suggest that the team put up a visible timetable that covers what the team needs to do to prepare for the demo. The team decides who will demonstrate each story—often this is agreed at the daily standup.

- Help the team avoid having technical glitches spoil the demo. Recommend the team sets up the room in advance and checks network connections. The team can even hold a rehearsal to make the demo really slick.

- Take notes on stakeholder reactions and feedback during the meeting. Review these feedback points with everyone before the meeting ends. Make sure the team captures this feedback as new user stories and takes them along to their next iteration planning session.

- As well as demonstrating working software in the iteration demo, the team agrees with the customer which stories meet their definition of "done" to calculate their final velocity.

- Encourage the team to automate both deployment and testing the deployment so releasing software can be done swiftly without errors.

- Celebrate the team's success after the demo. If things didn't go so well in the demo, discuss this in the retrospective, and work out actions with the team to avoid this the next time around.

Chapter 13

Driving Change with Retrospectives

Henrik Kniberg, author of *Scrum and XP from the Trenches* [Kni07], observes, "Without retrospectives you will find that the team keeps making the same mistakes over and over again." Like Bill Murray's character in the film *Groundhog Day*, the team can't break out of a painful cycle until they take the time to understand what happened and change their ways.

The retrospective provides a way for you to engage the team members in improving their process in direct response to problems that they face. As a coach, you want to enable the team to learn how to use their retrospective to identify where they feel pain in their current process and to learn how to reduce it themselves.

We often meet Agile teams that have already tried retrospectives and have given them up. They felt their retrospectives didn't result in any change so continuing with them was a waste of time. This situation is usually caused by not knowing how to run retrospectives. In this chapter, we'll explain some of the mechanics of retrospective design and share some techniques for running successful retrospectives.

13.1 Facilitating a Retrospective

It takes practice to get good at facilitating retrospectives; it helps to get clear on the underlying structure so you can help focus conversations on learning and improvements.

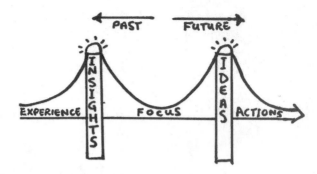

Figure 13.1: RETROSPECTIVES FORM A BRIDGE BETWEEN ITERATIONS

An iteration retrospective should help the team explore the following:

- What insights do they have from the last iteration?
- What areas do they want to focus on improving?
- What ideas can they act on in the next iteration?

Consider the retrospective as a bridge between the past iteration and future iterations, as illustrated in Figure 13.1. Spend half the retrospective looking back over the past iteration to uncover insights about what happened and why. Then shift into forward gear to come up with ideas to change things for the better and to develop action plans to implement the ideas.

You'll find that because retrospectives don't appear to connect directly with producing more software, there may be pressure to rush them—so the team can get back to their "real" work. However, skipping these steps—especially the last one—can prevent a retrospective from being effective.

It Takes Time
by Rachel

I joined a team that worked together for more than a year before trying a retrospective. We had plenty of problems building up but no meeting to air them within our XP process. When we finally held our first retrospective, we literally covered our board room table with issues written on index cards that needed to be fixed! It felt great to these out in the open, but it left us with a pile of work to do.

There were too many problems to fix in a single iteration; we fell back on our Agile planning techniques: we clustered the issues and prioritized them to find the worst problems. Our deployment and customer support processes were high on the list, so we started with those. Then we kept working on these issues and reviewing progress in retrospectives until gradually we solved them (or the problems went away).

This experience taught me that process improvement using retrospectives is iterative and can take a long time. Don't expect retrospectives to magically resolve all your problems straightaway.

In his book *Project Retrospectives* [Ker01], Norm Kerth encourages us to *get the story out* and then *mine for gold*—the gold is what we have learned by reflecting on what happened.

Looking Back

Buy-in from the team is needed for changes to stick. Build support for improvements by starting the retrospective with a review of what was learned in the last iteration—to get the story out.

Each person on the team has a different experience of past events. To understand what actually happened, the team needs to share their individual stories and integrate them. People will not feel like participating if they are not listened to, so ensure this part of the retrospective is not rushed. Take the time to hear what everyone has to say.

Our favorite way to do this is to create a timeline using sticky notes, as in Figure 13.2, on page 187. This helps the team piece together a complete picture of events. They'll also start to see how their actions were influenced by other things that were going on at the time. As events are added to the timeline, the team will start to remember other events and fill in the gaps. The timeline is a temporary artifact; you don't need to preserve it after the meeting.

When looking back, you may want to include a way for the team to indicate how they felt about the events. Here are some ways to do this:

Color timeline Use a scheme of different-colored sticky notes on the timeline to indicate feelings. Use green notes for events that were enjoyable, pink for stressful, and yellow for neutral. Post a key next to the timeline so it's clear what the colors mean. Don't forget to check whether everyone in the group can distinguish between the colors you're using before trying this.

Retrospective Smells

Here are some "smells" that indicate the retrospective isn't working:

Ideas fest The team members are asked to call out ideas *without* discussing what happened in the last iteration. This doesn't work because problems are glossed over. Actions may not be connected to resolving problems and tend to be about trying out cool stuff rather than fixing what's not working.

History lesson This retrospective is rather like an archaeological dig that results only in lists of "What Went Well" and "What Needs Improvement" but no actions. This can improve communication as the team gradually understands what's happening. But because there's no discussion about how to improve, change is left to individuals rather than planned into the next iteration.

Change the world The team commits to an ambitious list of actions without considering whether it has time to get them done in the next iteration. This leads to disappointment because the actions don't get done and the team adds more actions to this list every retrospective.

Wishful thinking Actions discussed are rather vague with no owners, such as "Improve communication" or "Do more refactoring." These are not actions; they are problems to work on. Without more discussion, the team doesn't really know what to do to implement these pseudoactions.

No time to improve The team takes five to ten minutes after their iteration demo to have a quick chat about how things have been going and calls that a retrospective. This is a sign that the team sees no benefit in retrospectives. If individuals do have ideas for improvement, then they face a struggle to implement them without a forum to get support from the team.

Hot air The team spends the retrospective grumbling about how bad things are without taking responsibility for improving the situation. This may be cathartic and release tension in the team but can easily turn into a blame game. Retrospectives are about making changes for the better, and that can't happen without some discussion of what the team *can* do.

Figure 13.2: Example of a timeline created with sticky notes

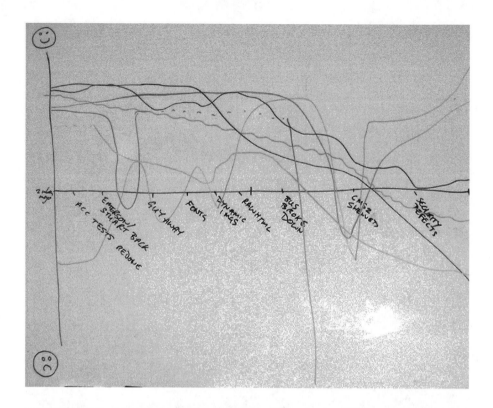

Figure 13.3: AN EMOTIONS SEISMOGRAPH DRAWN ON A WHITEBOARD

Emotions seismograph Invite the team to draw lines reflecting their mood over the iteration—an example is shown in Figure 13.3. This allows you to see how everyone was feeling at a certain time. And you can spot patterns when the whole team felt energized—or despondent.

Art gallery Ask the team to draw a picture of what the project felt like to them, and post these pictures on the wall in the meeting. Then give each person an opportunity to explain their drawing.[1]

Drawing pictures sounds odd, but doing this exercise can be used to surface serious topics. People are usually very good at finding metaphors for things that can be difficult to express in words. For example, one team member drew a picture of a stickman in a box.

---

1. Patrick Kua has a nice variant on this called "Mr. Squiggle." See http://www.thekua.com/atwork/2008/04/retrospective-exercise-mr-squiggle/.

When we asked him about it, he explained to his teammates that he had been working on his own too long and did not feel like he was part of the team anymore.

Mining for Gold

Now we need to draw out insights from the experience gained last iteration. Start by surveying the timeline to try to spot where to dig. To identify rich seams, walk the timeline, and read aloud each sticky note. If a note seems puzzling to you, invite the team to clarify, but do this carefully without demanding that the person who wrote the note explain it. Try digging down to underlying causes—if a task in the iteration went really well, what were the factors that enabled this? If you find general statements like "Testing environment broken" or "Customer too busy," ask for examples to illustrate the problem so the team can better understand the point being made.

If you use colored notes to indicate feelings of the team, you will also see patterns where notes of the same color tend to bunch together around key events. The peaks and troughs of mood lines on an *emotions seismograph* do the same. These can show differences in how the iteration was experienced by different roles. For example, you might see all the developers draw positive lines toward the end of the iteration because they finished all their tasks, but maybe a tester draws a more negative line because he had all the testing dumped on him on the final day of the iteration. Draw the team's attention to the diverging lines to prompt them to discuss what's happening here.

After you've walked the timeline, the team needs to choose the most important topics to focus on. Whittle this list down to the team's top two or three topics using *dot voting*. Each team member gets three votes that they cast by drawing dots next to the topics they want to discuss most. They can spread their dots between topics, or they can put more than one dot if a topic is more important to them than all the rest. Tally the dots after everyone has voted to identify what topics to take forward into action planning.

Once you have extracted the topics the team wants to focus on, shift into looking forward for process improvements the team can make in the next iteration.

Rachel Says...

Introduce the Elephant in the Room

Professor Randy Pausch started his Last Lecture* by saying, "My father always said, 'When there's an elephant in the room, introduce them!' " He went on to explain that he had only a few months left to live, and although we cannot change the cards we are dealt, we get to decide how respond and how we play the hand.

If you have the feeling that the team is skirting around an issue in a retrospective, don't be afraid to raise it. Create an opportunity to talk about it, but move on if the team members aren't ready to discuss it.

*. http://www.cmu.edu/randyslecture/

Looking Forward

The second half of the retrospective looks forward to the next iteration. This is when the team works out what they'd like to change about their process. But you'll need more than agreement that changes are necessary; the team must work out actions to implement the changes. And the actions need to get done!

Before starting to create new actions in the retrospective, take the time to review what happened on the actions from the last retrospective. If those actions have not been completed, then the team needs to understand why before piling on more actions. Often, the reason actions have not been completed is that they were poorly defined or had no clear owner. But it's also quite common for teams not to get the actions done because they didn't have time.

Allow plenty of time in the retrospective to work out a realistic plan of action that's clear to everyone on the team. For actions to get done, the team also needs time to complete them. Before deciding any actions, work out with the team how much of their time in the next iteration they can dedicate to process improvements while continuing to develop software.

Action Shoes

There's a rather quirky book by Edward De Bono called *Six Action Shoes* (Bon93) that we like because it makes clear that there are different sorts of actions by likening them to different types of shoes. These are as follows:

- Orange gumboots for quick fixes to resolve an immediate emergency
- Brown brogues for practical action
- Gray sneakers for gathering more data about a problem
- Navy formal shoes for actions that need to follow a standard process
- Purple boots for actions that require authority
- Pink fluffy slippers for situations that require care for people's feelings

Taking Baby Steps

So, how do you get to new actions that are achievable? Well, if you can identify a problem or an aspirational goal, then you can ask the team what the baby steps are toward it. The smaller these action steps are, the more likely it is that the team can get them done. With each suggested action step, check whether anything else needs to happen before they can get started. If there is another activity, then that also needs to be an action.

Actions are not always about fixing a problem (see the sidebar on the current page for ideas about different types of actions). You need to understand a problem before you can fix it, so the team may need to start with actions to explore the problem and gather data. For example, if the team is worried about time being lost due to interruptions, they can make a start by tracking how often the interruptions are happening and where they come from. Or if the build is very slow, they can create an action to change the code to output some timestamps to help pinpoint the problem. When you have more data, you can work out actions that directly address the problem. You may also need actions to see whether the changes have resolved the problem. Also, after you've found a solution that works well, you may want to let other teams know about it and create actions around sharing lessons learned.

To create actions that will stick, it's not enough to identify *what* needs to happen; the team also needs to agree on *how* the changes will be implemented. Rachel has facilitated some retrospectives with Bas Vodde who uses a special technique for action planning.[2] This can be especially effective in groups that take a passive stance to retrospectives because they are used to managers deciding actions for them.

Here's the basic process:

1. Ask each team member to work on their own to write a list of actions that they would like the team to take.

2. Next the team works in pairs to combine their lists into a consolidated shortlist.

3. Then the pairs join up with other pairs to further reduce their lists.

4. Eventually the team has a shortlist of actions that have been refined by the whole group.

Once you have a set of actions that the whole team is happy with, you can wrap up the meeting. Don't forget that, after the retrospective, these actions need to be considered when planning the next iteration. Post the actions on the team board so they aren't forgotten during the next iteration.

Out of Sight, Out of Mind
by Rachel

When facilitating a retrospective with a team recently, Rachel asked the team for the list of past actions. The team leader had to leave the meeting room to retrieve them from his desk drawer. Needless to say, none of the actions had been started. We find teams that post their actions on their team board are more likely to complete them!

13.2 Designing a Retrospective

Guidelines for running effective meetings (see Section 3.4, *Facilitating Meetings*, on page 43) apply to retrospectives too. You'll need to do some basic preparation, such as booking a room and making sure you bring a supply of marker pens and sticky notes. But the hardest bit is usually working out the agenda.

---

2. Read "Plan of Action" by Bas Vodde online at http://www.scrumalliance.org/articles/61-plan-of-action.

You can suggest different activities to the team to help them:

- Reveal insights

- Agree on a focus for process improvement

- Enable creative problem solving

Decide how long you will need for the retrospective based on iteration length, how many people are in the team, and whether any remote team members will be included. New teams usually need a little bit more time. So, for instance, if iterations are two weeks long, we recommend you allow ninety minutes for up to ten team members (who can all attend the meeting in person). Of course, you don't have to use up all the time; it's fine to finish early!

Here's an example of how to break down the time:

- Review the goal of meeting, and remind the team of the ground rules (5 minutes).

- Create a timeline (15 minutes).

- Mine the timeline for insights (15 minutes).

- Select the topics to focus on (10 minutes).

- Review the progress on previous actions (5 minutes).

- Generate ideas for improvements (15 minutes).

- Action planning (15 minutes).

This is a good format to start with, but using the same meeting format every time becomes boring for the team. So, vary the format; Esther Derby and Diana Larsen describe an excellent selection of alternative activities that you can use in retrospectives in *Agile Retrospectives* [DL06].

Prime Directive

As with any meeting, you need some basic ground rules, such as no laptops, switching phones to silent, and taking turns to speak. However, there's one special ground rule that underpins all retrospectives called the *prime directive* (from *Project Retrospectives* [Ker01]). This states that "Regardless of what we discover, we understand and truly believe that everyone did the best job they could, given what they knew at the time, their skills and abilities, the resources available, and the situation at hand."

Make it safe to explore what went wrong.

People learn more from exploring real situations where mistakes were made than studying best practice. Setting the prime directive as a ground rule helps to make it safe to explore what went wrong because it points us at the situational causes of action and absolves the people in the situation from blame.

This may sound a bit naive! Surely, there are times when people slipped up and made mistakes? Although the prime directive seems to deny that some problems can be caused by individuals, it's better understood as making clear that retrospectives are not the best place to discuss individual performance issues. Following this directive, you steer the conversation away from the blame and destructive criticism that can damage teamwork. Retrospectives should focus instead on how to improve team process; if individual performance comes up, shift the focus back onto team actions.

The prime directive also helps counter *fundamental attribution error*, which is the human tendency to explain the actions of other people as deliberate choice and downplay the situational factors. For instance, a developer might complain that a tester copied the QA manager on an email because "she wanted to get the team into trouble" rather than understanding that there were other factors in play. In fact, she had been asked by her line manager to copy him on all her emails and was doing this routinely, not vindictively.

People also like to be consistent with their past actions. By framing previous action and decisions as reasonable at the time (given the situation), the prime directive frees up discussion about doing things differently the next time. In other words, it won't be inconsistent to behave differently because the situation will be different.

We recommend that the first time you run a retrospective, you post the prime directive on the wall and explain it to the team. If the conversation starts getting too negative, then you can remind the team to think about the situational forces at work rather than blaming individuals.

13.3 Broader Retrospectives

While iteration retrospectives focus on more immediate problems affecting the team, there will be issues outside the team that can't be resolved in their team retrospectives. This is a sign that you need to run a retrospective with a broader focus to look at the bigger picture. These broader retrospectives look back over several iterations with a larger group. This meeting will include people who work with the team, such as sales, marketing, customer support, operational support, and system administrators. A good time to hold these retrospectives is after a major software release, so they're often called *release retrospectives*.

Larger retrospectives often include management and people who don't work together on a daily basis, so conversations might be less free flowing, which makes them harder to facilitate. Focus your efforts on getting good at running iteration retrospectives, before trying retrospectives with a larger group, to help you practice facilitation with a more manageable group size. If you don't feel confident to lead such a large or diverse group, consider bringing in an independent facilitator.

Most of the techniques used in retrospectives with the team, such as the timeline, can also be used in larger retrospectives. The big difference is that you will be working with a larger group that may not be as comfortable discussing issues as the team might be. You may need to include a *safety check*; this is an anonymous ballot to see how comfortable the group is with talking about issues arising from the past period of work. It can also be more productive to break into subgroups to discuss topics and then present back to the whole group.

Another difference is that you will be looking back over a longer period of time. For a retrospective that looks back over many months, some prework is needed—you need to do some digging so you can provide the team with reminders of what happened. Bring along to the retrospective reminders of what stories were worked on, and print some reference copies of key project artifacts such as release burn charts or wiki pages. For larger groups, it may also be useful to send an email survey to collect the issues that they want to raise (see the sidebar on the next page).

13.4 Hurdles

The following are some hurdles you may encounter.

Same Actions Come Up

Often the same action comes up again and again. This is usually caused by not splitting the actions down into tasks that can be achieved in a single iteration. It helps to set a long-term goal and then create a list of short-term steps toward the goal. For example, if Continuous Integration is the goal, then installing tools, configuring tools, and preparing test suites could be separate actions.

Retrospective Prework

Here's an example of a survey we have sent out to participants before the retrospective to collect the issues they want to discuss:

To help me work out the best format for the retrospective, I would appreciate if you would send me an email answering the following questions:

- *For you, what are the top three topics that need to be discussed?*
- *Looking back, are there any high points that stand out for you?*
- *Were there any particular events that are still a puzzle for you?*
- *What reservations or concerns do you have about this retrospective?*
- *What impact do you hope this retrospective will have?*

Your answers will be kept in strict confidence. I will review everyone's comments and identify common themes, but no individual response will be shared with the group.

If even small actions do not get done, the team needs to discuss why. There needs to be capacity every iteration for getting these done; otherwise, there's not much point in having retrospectives!

Silent Team Members

You may find some team members who are quiet because they don't feel comfortable talking in a group. Often programmers are introverts; plan the retrospective to include writing activities to encourage their input. You might also experiment with round-robin discussion, inviting an opinion from each team member in turn. However, make it clear that it's OK to say, "Pass."

Team Is Always Moaning

Sometimes a retrospective turns into a moaning session. The team becomes overly focused on complaining rather than constructive discussion. It's usually about issues that the team perceives as being outside their sphere of influence. If the complaints are focused on a specific incident that impacted them, such as servers not being available, talking about the incident may help clear the air. But try to get the team back into learning mode by asking, "If this situation happens again, how should we react to it?" Maybe there are additional checks that the team can make before starting a piece of work. Or perhaps they can track how much time they are losing and flag this up to management.

Staying Neutral

When you have been working on the team, you probably want to share your own impressions about past events and get involved in brainstorming actions. This is hard to do if you are supposed to be running the meeting. You also need to be careful not to be seen as "taking sides," "playing favorites," or abusing your position as meeting facilitator to get more airtime for your own favorite topics. If you work alongside other agile teams, suggest taking turns facilitating retrospectives for one another's teams; this way you can be a participant of your own team's retrospective. Otherwise, you could rotate the facilitation role within the team.

13.5 Checklist

- Start the retrospective by looking back to understand what happened and why. Allow enough time for the team to tell the full story.

- Spend the second half of the retrospective looking forward and deciding on a plan of action.

- Watch out for retrospective "smells" that are stopping your team's retrospectives from being effective. If the retrospectives aren't driving process improvement, think about how you could run them better.

- Find out what problems the team wants to fix most. Use dot voting to focus on what the team has energy to work on.

- Don't commit to more actions than can be completed before the next retrospective. Even two or three actions completed every iteration can have significant impact over several months.

- If the actions from last retrospective weren't done, find out why before adding any more.

Chapter 14

Growing You

We've spent most of the book talking about how you can help your team, so now we're going to talk about you. It's vital to invest in yourself and in your own learning so you can grow as a person and keep your ideas fresh. You also need to take care of yourself in order to cope with the day-to-day demands of being an Agile coach.

As a coach, you're constantly leading change, so it's important to be open to change yourself. Take the time to reflect on your own performance and experiences and learn from them rather than repeating the same mistakes. Expose yourself to new ideas. Seek out ways to develop and grow.

14.1 Ways to Grow What You Know

You can learn by reading books, articles, magazines, or websites. You can listen to podcasts, talk to people, or learn by doing. There are many online discussions, newsgroups, and webinars that you can participate in.

Work out how you learn best, and set aside time to do it. Here are some ideas to get you started:

- Commit to read one technical book per month.
- Start your own blog.
- Contribute to an open source project.
- Post once a day to a community mailing list.
- Listen to a podcast on your way to work.
- Spare one evening a month to attend an interest group.

You may want to research a single topic deeply and read multiple books on that topic. Or go for breadth of knowledge, and cover several topics in a week by timeboxing your learning. You'll be surprised how much you can learn in an hour.

The greater the variety of material you expose yourself to, the more you will learn. Improving a team's performance is not unique to software development. Add to your repertoire by learning how other industries approach similar problems. Read widely from multiple fields including coaching, management, and psychology.

Share What You Learned

Share what you learn with others to consolidate your learning. Look for an opportunity to give a presentation about your topic either at work or to a special interest group. You'll find that preparing your talk reinforces your learning. Delivering the talk gives you confidence that you really have learned it.

It is fine to open your presentation by saying that you are not an expert on this topic and inviting suggestions from the audience if they have something to contribute. After the talk, extend your learning by following up on questions people ask you.

Get Some Training

There are some excellent training courses on coaching, facilitation, leadership, and interpersonal skills. Training courses provide a chance to role play and try new skills in a safe environment, where it is OK to make a mistake and where you won't cause offense.

There are also certifications you can get in coaching and in facilitation, such as the International Association of Facilitators (IAF) Certified Professional Facilitator qualification. Certification requires in-depth knowledge of a topic and can provide you with confidence that you are doing things properly.

Speak with Ease
by Liz

A few years ago, I was going through a bad spell. I'd left a job that had ended badly, and it had taken a while—and many job interviews—to find my next job. My confidence at work was very low. I no longer felt comfortable talking freely to people more senior than me.

Rachel Says...

Remembering What You Read

I read a lot of technical books, and I want to remember the key points. There are some techniques that can help.

One technique, recommended to me by Linda Rising, is to keep a card in the back of the book, and as you read, note down interesting quotes and ideas with page numbers. After you finish reading the book, consolidate by writing a summary of what you learned from the book. Later you can pick up the book, flip to the summary you wrote, and find the bits you want to reference quickly.

Another technique is described by Tony Buzan in *Use Your Head* (Buz03). Instead of starting at the front of the book and working through to the back, approach the book as you would work on a jigsaw puzzle. Examine the pieces, sort them into similar piles, find the corners, and build the edges. Fill in easy bits first and difficult bits last with careful reference to the big picture on the box.

Before you start reading the book, create a mindmap of what you already know about the subject. Get clear about your goals and questions to be answered by reading the book. Now follow these reading steps:

- *Overview:* Browse the book to get an idea of structure by looking at all material not in main body of print, such as the figures, glossary, and so on.

- *Preview:* Read just the introductions and summaries for each chapter to build an understanding of the book's main points.

- *Inview:* Read the content to fill in your understanding, skipping any difficult sections.

- *Review:* Check through the remainder of the book.

Add to your mindmap as you go. When you go back to the book months or years later, your mindmap will help you recall what you learned.

On a whim I decided to join Toastmasters.[1] Every week I went to a pub where we gave prepared speeches and critiqued each other.

I was very nervous giving my first speech. I was advised to speak about myself, so I told a personal story. The speech came across well, and I got loads of positive feedback. My confidence started to grow.

For the next two years, I went regularly to Toastmasters. I learned that if your tale comes from your heart, it will come across well. I learned you need to speak with passion to win people over. I also learned how to give constructive criticism to others, how to find some good points and some bad points about everybody's speech, and how to present that information to them.

This was a great place to practice in a safe environment, and my confidence blossomed. Soon I was so comfortable with public speaking that I started to apply to speak at conferences.

I would recommend Toastmasters to anyone, because improving the way you speak, learning how to give and to receive feedback, and learning how to convince people of your view are invaluable lessons. Plus you'll make good friends and have a great time.

14.2 Making a Plan

We recommend you create your own personal development plan. Think hard about what you like about your job and where your interests lie. Set some personal goals and objectives to take you along on the development path you choose. You'll also need to consider how much time and money you are prepared to spend implementing your plan.

We are often surprised by the attitude of many employees to professional development. When we suggest reading a book or attending a seminar, the usual response is "I will if I can get my employer to pay for it," and if the employer won't cough up, then it seems this is completely out of the question. We recommend you challenge this attitude. In the software industry, it is rare to have a job for life. How can you expect your employer to invest in your development if you are not prepared to do the same? Do you really want to be pushed down a career path rather than taking responsibility for building the experience to support where you want to go?

---

1. http://www.toastmasters.org/

Don't go overboard. Bear in mind other commitments; your plan needs to be achievable. If you're self-employed, it's fairly straightforward to allocate a budget for buying books, attending conferences, and getting training. If you're an employee, share your plans for personal development with your line manager. Demonstrating that you are prepared to invest some of your own time and money will show how serious you are, which can help convince your manager to back you with more funds. Whether you get financial backing or not, we're sure that you won't regret it—learning is its own reward.

14.3 Building Your Network

Meeting up with other people who care about Agile and care about software helps you reset your compass. Explaining your frustrations to others is a relief but also helps to put things into perspective. Other people will have different ideas, experiences, and points of view that can challenge your thinking.

Often you are so deeply involved in your own company that it is hard to see the forest for the trees, but when you listen to others, things jump out at you. You'll also find that listening to other people's frustrations and suggesting ideas for them to try is great practice for coaching.

Don't just focus on the Agile software community. Seek out coaches or facilitators who work in other industries, who can help you develop those skills, and who gain perspective on your current job role.

Conferences

There are a lot of conferences devoted to Agile software development, large and small.

Attending at least one a year is a great way to gain new ideas and insights. It is also a way to connect with the wider Agile community.

As well as learning from the sessions, most people find they have useful insights when mingling with the other attendees in between sessions or at the pub afterward. There are also Agile unconferences[2] that encourage participants to create their own conference agenda; you're welcome to propose a session on a topic that interests you.

---

2. http://www.agileopen.net/

You'll get even more out of the experience if you contribute to a conference by presenting a workshop or experience report. When you prepare for your session, you'll learn more about your chosen topic. Then when you present it, you'll likely meet people who share your interests. Being a presenter also makes the conference more affordable, because registration for presenters is often subsidized or free.

Conference Junkie
by Rachel

I love going to conferences and meeting up with experts and practitioners face-to-face to hear all the latest new ideas. I've also discovered I love organizing conferences. This started with XPDay back in 2001, and last year I chaired Agile 2008 conference in Toronto with 400 sessions and 1,600 attendees. Through doing this I've learned a lot about leading distributed teams.

You don't need to go as far as running Agile events; simply being a reviewer is an eye-opening experience. You get to see how decisions are made about what is selected for the program or not. This helps you improve your own session proposals the next time around.

User Groups

Another great way to share ideas and get support is to go to a local Agile interest group. These groups normally meet weekly or monthly in pubs or company offices. Some groups have presentations by speakers, while others are more informal.

User groups exist in most major cities around the world.[3] Because they are local to you, this is a place where you can meet people who will become friends or mentors and people who can help you regularly over a long time.

Mailing lists and online forums are another way to get involved. Yahoo, Google, and LinkedIn all have active Agile groups. You will get much more out of these online communities if you participate rather than just lurk. Reading conversations helps you learn, and replying to questions posed makes you think through the problem more deeply. Phrasing your answer constructively allows you to practice coaching people in different situations.

---

3. See http://www.agilealliance.org/usergroups.

14.4 Personal Reflections

Reflect on experiences you have had, and think about how recent experiences are linked to earlier ones to see connections and learn from them. If you did something that worked, what was it you did? Why did it work? Would it work again? When your actions don't have the effect you intended, what went wrong? How might you approach a similar situation next time?

Keep a Journal

Consider writing a journal either daily or weekly. This is a very good way of reflecting on your performance and improving it.

> **My Journal**
> *by Liz*
>
> I like to spend the first half hour of my working day in a closed office writing my journal and reading yesterday's entries. I find it impossible to think deeply and write my journal at my desk in the middle of an open plan office, because it is not private and because writing my journal involves a lot of staring into space and chewing my pen.

Writing down your thoughts helps you think about recent situations and how you feel about how you handled them. As you examine your behavior, you reflect on alternatives ways you could have acted. Force yourself to write at

> Write down your thoughts to help articulate your feelings.

least three pages, because you need to write more than just the obvious, surface layer reactions for a journal to be powerful. Writing a journal is not always easy. Sometimes it is very painful to articulate what you are feeling, and it's painful to be honest and realize where problems stem from.

Read your journal periodically, and you will be surprised how far you have come. Patterns you didn't notice at the time might now be obvious. With hindsight, you may be surprised by your initial reactions and thoughts. You may be kinder to your past self and realize that it wasn't all your fault—that there were other contributing factors.

Success Journal

A useful variation on a journal is a *success journal* where you write only about the things you've done well. Reflect on all the good things you've done, rather than constantly criticizing yourself. Over time this can be a hugely effective tool, because you gain confidence and realize you are doing an awful lot of things right. Keep in mind that *you get what you focus on.*

Success breeds success, problems breed problems.

This is part of an approach called *appreciative inquiry*, which can be applied in many situations. The basic idea is to build organizations around what works, rather than trying to fix what doesn't. For instance, you could run a retrospective where the team discusses only what is going well.

Of course, the following advice also applies: "If you do what you've always done, you'll get what you've always gotten."[4] Find a balance between focusing on your strengths (and how you can use them more) and looking at what else needs to improve. Keep in mind that very successful people tend to spend most of their time doing things that they are good at.

Get a Coach

Talking to someone else often enables you to solve your own problems. They may see how your actions led you into a situation more easily than you can. And if they are experienced and tactful in how they lead you to consider past mistakes, you are more likely to learn from them.

It's also good to turn the tables and experience being a *coachee*. Not only will you learn tips and techniques on how to coach, but you will also learn what it feels like to be coached. If done properly, you'll find it invigorating and empowering; but done poorly, you may find it aggravating and that it reinforces resistance.

If there is no one suitable at work who could be your coach, you might find someone at your local user group or at a conference. It is possible to find a coach who can work with you over the phone and by email, but it is better if you can meet up once a month for lunch or similar. Discuss what happened over the last month, what the highlights were, and what mistakes you're concerned about, as well as what you learned and what you still want to learn.

Set stretch goals for the next month, preferably SMART[5] goals that can be achieved within a month. A personal trainer can push you further

---

4. Quote from Anthony Robbins.
5. Specific, Measurable, Achievable, Realistic and Timely

than you can push yourself, and a respected coach can do the same by challenging you.

Take a Break

Take time in your day to reflect. Going for a walk is an excellent time to think about how things are going and planning for the future. Swimming, walking, running, yoga, or even a hot bath are all excellent ways to reflect and unwind. The important thing is that you are not interrupted so you can relax and let your mind drift. Dreaming about the future is an important step to making it happen. Thoughts need time to make it from your subconscious to your conscious. You need time to talk to yourself.

If you don't take time to unwind, you will be unable to put events into perspective and context. If you are stressed, everything seems bigger, worse, and more important than it really is.

Try to get a sense of perspective. What are you stressed about? When you look back a year from now, will it still seem important? If not, then is it important enough to worry about now?

We like this quote from Edith Seashore: "Someday, We'll look back on this and laugh. Why not now?"[6]

14.5 Getting Comfortable

To be an Agile coach, you need to develop a thick skin; you can't get upset when people don't follow your advice. Not everybody appreciates being challenged and stretched, and they may try to take it out on you.

Be Kind

As well as being kind to yourself, don't judge others harshly. Always assume everyone is doing their best and that they do everything for a reason. Now, their best may not be great for a variety of reasons, and you may not understand their motivation for behaving the way they do. So, try to find out. Don't guess and then judge and gossip. Go talk to them, find out about them—you may be surprised.

Like the old saying goes, "Don't judge someone until you have walked a mile in their shoes." There are all sorts of reasons why people's behavior

---

6. Personal communication from Gerald M. Weinberg

Liz Says...

Be Kind to Yourself

I was at a conference once, complaining to someone I respected about all the mistakes I was making at work and how hard it was to coach a team. She just looked at me and said:

"And you don't think anyone else makes mistakes?"

"Well, no. I guess everyone makes mistakes."

"So why are you being so hard on yourself?"

"Because..." a hundred reasons ran through my mind like: I'm meant to be good, it's embarrassing to make obvious mistakes, I want to do better.

"Be kind to yourself," she said.

That really struck me. Like most people, I am very harsh on myself. Expecting myself not to make mistakes, to do better, to always be competent. Why not be kind to myself? When my son makes a mistake, I give him a hug, tell him to not worry, and tell him next time he'll do better. Why don't I do that to myself?

---

deteriorates at work. Their personal life may be going through a rocky patch, or they may be worried about losing their job. They may feel like they have to compromise their values or are being pushed beyond their comfort zone. If you have never performed badly at work, consider yourself very lucky. You have probably not been placed in an overly stressful situation.

The Road Ahead

Don't let your job grow stale. If you feel you have outgrown your current role, there may be other opportunities within your company.

- Can you move to a new team, project, or department?
- Can you coach more people than before?
- Can you coach different job roles than you have been doing?
- Can you mentor someone else?

We hope you've found this book a useful guide to being an Agile coach and that it takes you to interesting places. Our parting words to you are these: keep a eye on the road ahead to ensure your career is running the way you want it to run. Make sure your work is always challenging, preferably just a little too hard for you so you stay engaged.

14.6 Checklist

- Make time to learn. Create a plan of what you want to learn this month and for how you will do so.
- Make time to reflect. The most powerful lessons don't come from books but from learning from our own mistakes—small or large.
- Take time out to destress. Work can seem very important, and it is easy to let it swallow you up. Keep things in perspective by making time for yourself every day.
- Meet other people who care about the same things as you. Local interest groups and conferences are great places to meet people who will help you keep your passion for Agile alive.
- Be kind to yourself. Forgive your mistakes. Learn from them, make amends, and move on.
- Be kind to others. Don't attribute bad intentions to people. Instead, find out why they are acting that way. Differences in opinion and style in a team are good.
- Don't let your job grow stale. Keep pushing yourself at work; otherwise, it will no longer be fun.

Appendix A

Bibliography

[Bec00]   Kent Beck. Extreme leadership: Celebrate accomplishment. File on Extreme Programming discussion list, 2000.

[Bec07]   Kent Beck. *Implementation Patterns*. Addison-Wesley, Reading, MA, 2007.

[Bel05]   Arlo Belshee. Promiscuous pairing and beginner's mind: Embrace inexperience. *Proceedings of the Agile 2005 conference*, pages 125–131, July 2005.

[Bon93]   Edward De Bono. *Six Action Shoes*. HarperCollins Publishers Ltd, London, 1993.

[Buz03]   Tony Buzan. *Use Your Head*. BBC Active, London, UK, 2003.

[Coh06]   Mike Cohn. *Agile Estimating and Planning*. Prentice Hall, Englewood Cliffs, NJ, 2006.

[DL06]   Esther Derby and Diana Larsen. *Agile Retrospectives: Making Good Teams Great*. The Pragmatic Programmers, LLC, Raleigh, NC, and Dallas, TX, 2006.

[Eme01]   Dale H. Emery. Resistance as a resource. File on website, 2001.

[Fea04]   Michael Feathers. *Working Effectively with Legacy Code*. Prentice Hall, Englewood Cliffs, NJ, 2004.

[Gre]   James Grenning. Planning poker or how to avoid analysis paralysis while release planning. http://www.renaissancesoftware.net/files/articles/PlanningPoker-v1.1.pdf.

[Her93]   Frederick Herzberg. *The Motivation to Work*. Transaction Publishers, Piscataway, New Jersey, 1993.

[Hil]   Linda A Hill. *Becoming a Manager*. Harvard Business School Press, Boston.

[HMMP]   Julian Higman, Tim Mackinnon, Ivan Moore, and Duncan Pierce. Innovation and sustainability with gold cards. http://www.agilealliance.com/system/article/file/999/file.pdf.

[HT00]   Andrew Hunt and David Thomas. *The Pragmatic Programmer: From Journeyman to Master*. Addison-Wesley, Reading, MA, 2000.

[Hun08]   Andy Hunt. *Pragmatic Thinking & Learning: Refactor Your Wetware*. The Pragmatic Programmers, LLC, Raleigh, NC, and Dallas, TX, 2008.

[Jan82]   Irving L. Janis. *Group Think*. Houghton Mifflin, Boston, Massachusetts, 1982.

[Jef]   Ron Jeffries. Essential XP: Card, conversation, confirmation. http://www.xprogramming.com/xpmag/expCardConversationConfirmation.htm.

[Ker01]   Norman L. Kerth. *Project Retrospectives: A Handbook for Team Reviews*. Dorset House, New York, 2001.

[KLT⁺96]   Sam Kaner, Lenny Lind, Catherine Toldi, Sarah Fisk, and Duane Berger. *The Facilitator's Guide to Participatory Decision-Making*. New Society Publishers, Gabriola Island, BC, 1996.

[Kni07]   Henrik Kniberg. *Scrum and XP from the Trenches*. InfoQ, Toronto, 2007.

[Koh93]   Alfie Kohn. *Punished by Rewards: The Trouble with Gold Stars, Incentive Plans, A's, Praise, and Other Bribes*. Houghton Mifflin Company, Boston, 1993.

[Len05]   Patrick Lencioni. *Overcoming the Five Dysfunctions of a Team: A Field Guide*. Jossey-Bass, A Wiley Company, San Francisco, 2005.

[Lit03]   Jim Little. Change your organization (for peons). *Proceedings of the 2003 Agile Development Conference*, pages 54–59, June 2003.

[LV09]   Craig Larman and Bas Vodde. *Scaling Lean and Agile Development*. Addison-Wesley, Reading, MA, 2009.

[Mar08]   Robert C. Martin. *Clean Code: A Handbook of Agile Software Craftsmanship*. Prentice Hall, Englewood Cliffs, NJ, 2008.

[MR04]   Mary Lynn Manns and Linda Rising. *Fearless Change: Patterns for Introducing New Ideas*. Addison-Wesley, Reading, MA, 2004.

[Nor06]   Dan North. Behavior modification. *Better Software*, March, 2006.

[Ohn88]   Taiichi Ohno. *Toyota Production System: Beyond Large Scale Production*. Productivity Press, New York, 1988.

[PP06]   Mary Poppendieck and Tom Poppendieck. *Implementing Lean Software Development: From Concept to Cash*. Addison-Wesley, Reading, MA, 2006.

[Roc06]   David Rock. *Quiet Leadership*. Harpercollins, New York, 2006.

[Ros03]   Marshall Rosenberg. *Nonviolent Communication: a Language of Life*. Puddle Dancer Press, Encinitas, CA, 2003.

[Wak04]   William C. Wake. *Refactoring Workbook*. Addison-Wesley, Reading, MA, 2004.

[Wei85]   Gerald M. Weinberg. *The Secrets of Consulting*. Dorset House, New York, 1985.

Index

The Pragmatic Bookshelf

Available in paperback and DRM-free PDF, our titles are here to help you stay on top of your game. The following are in print as of July 2009; be sure to check our website at pragprog.com for newer titles.

Title	Year	ISBN	Pages
Advanced Rails Recipes: 84 New Ways to Build Stunning Rails Apps	2008	9780978739225	464
Agile Retrospectives: Making Good Teams Great	2006	9780977616640	200
Agile Web Development with Rails, Third Edition	2009	9781934356166	784
Augmented Reality: A Practical Guide	2008	9781934356036	328
Behind Closed Doors: Secrets of Great Management	2005	9780976694021	192
Best of Ruby Quiz	2006	9780976694076	304
Core Animation for Mac OS X and the iPhone: Creating Compelling Dynamic User Interfaces	2008	9781934356104	200
Data Crunching: Solve Everyday Problems using Java, Python, and More	2005	9780974514079	208
Deploying Rails Applications: A Step-by-Step Guide	2008	9780978739201	280
Design Accessible Web Sites: 36 Keys to Creating Content for All Audiences and Platforms	2007	9781934356029	336
Desktop GIS: Mapping the Planet with Open Source Tools	2008	9781934356067	368
Developing Facebook Platform Applications with Rails	2008	9781934356128	200
Enterprise Integration with Ruby	2006	9780976694069	360
Enterprise Recipes with Ruby and Rails	2008	9781934356234	416
Everyday Scripting with Ruby: for Teams, Testers, and You	2007	9780977616619	320
FXRuby: Create Lean and Mean GUIs with Ruby	2008	9781934356074	240
From Java To Ruby: Things Every Manager Should Know	2006	9780976694090	160
GIS for Web Developers: Adding Where to Your Web Applications	2007	9780974514093	275
Google Maps API, V2: Adding Where to Your Applications	2006	PDF-Only	83
Groovy Recipes: Greasing the Wheels of Java	2008	9780978739294	264
Hello, Android: Introducing Google's Mobile Development Platform	2008	9781934356173	200
Interface Oriented Design	2006	9780976694052	240
Land the Tech Job You Love	2009	9781934356265	280

Continued on next page

Title	Year	ISBN	Pages
Learn to Program, 2nd Edition	2009	9781934356364	230
Manage It! Your Guide to Modern Pragmatic Project Management	2007	9780978739249	360
Mastering Dojo: JavaScript and Ajax Tools for Great Web Experiences	2008	9781934356111	568
Modular Java: Creating Flexible Applications with OSGi and Spring	2009	9781934356401	260
No Fluff Just Stuff 2006 Anthology	2006	9780977616664	240
No Fluff Just Stuff 2007 Anthology	2007	9780978739287	320
Practical Programming: An Introduction to Computer Science Using Python	2009	9781934356272	350
Practices of an Agile Developer	2006	9780974514086	208
Pragmatic Project Automation: How to Build, Deploy, and Monitor Java Applications	2004	9780974514031	176
Pragmatic Thinking and Learning: Refactor Your Wetware	2008	9781934356050	288
Pragmatic Unit Testing in C# with NUnit	2007	9780977616671	176
Pragmatic Unit Testing in Java with JUnit	2003	9780974514017	160
Pragmatic Version Control Using Git	2008	9781934356159	200
Pragmatic Version Control using CVS	2003	9780974514000	176
Pragmatic Version Control using Subversion	2006	9780977616657	248
Programming Clojure	2009	9781934356333	304
Programming Erlang: Software for a Concurrent World	2007	9781934356005	536
Programming Groovy: Dynamic Productivity for the Java Developer	2008	9781934356098	320
Programming Ruby: The Pragmatic Programmers' Guide, Second Edition	2004	9780974514055	864
Programming Ruby 1.9: The Pragmatic Programmers' Guide	2009	9781934356081	960
Programming Scala: Tackle Multi-Core Complexity on the Java Virtual Machine	2009	9781934356319	250
Prototype and script.aculo.us: You Never Knew JavaScript Could Do This!	2007	9781934356012	448
Rails Recipes	2006	9780977616602	350
Rails for .NET Developers	2008	9781934356203	300
Rails for Java Developers	2007	9780977616695	336
Rails for PHP Developers	2008	9781934356043	432
Rapid GUI Development with QtRuby	2005	PDF-Only	83
Release It! Design and Deploy Production-Ready Software	2007	9780978739218	368
Scripted GUI Testing with Ruby	2008	9781934356180	192
Ship it! A Practical Guide to Successful Software Projects	2005	9780974514048	224

Continued on next page

Title	Year	ISBN	Pages
Stripes ...and Java Web Development Is Fun Again	2008	9781934356210	375
TextMate: Power Editing for the Mac	2007	9780978739232	208
The Definitive ANTLR Reference: Building Domain-Specific Languages	2007	9780978739256	384
The Passionate Programmer: Creating a Remarkable Career in Software Development	2009	9781934356340	200
ThoughtWorks Anthology	2008	9781934356142	240
Ubuntu Kung Fu: Tips, Tricks, Hints, and Hacks	2008	9781934356227	400

Agile Practices

Practices of an Agile Developer

Agility is all about using feedback to respond to change. Learn how to • apply the principles of agility throughout the software development process • establish and maintain an agile working environment • deliver what users really want • use personal agile techniques for better coding and debugging • use effective collaborative techniques for better teamwork • move to an agile approach

Practices of an Agile Developer:
Working in the Real World
Venkat Subramaniam and Andy Hunt
(189 pages) ISBN: 0-9745140-8-X. $29.95
http://pragprog.com/titles/pad

Ship It!

Page after page of solid advice, all tried and tested in the real world. This book offers a collection of tips that show you what tools a successful team has to use, and how to use them well. You'll get quick, easy-to-follow advice on modern techniques and when they should be applied. **You need this book if:** • you're frustrated at lack of progress on your project. • you want to make yourself and your team more valuable. • you've looked at methodologies such as Extreme Programming (XP) and felt they were too, well, extreme. • you've looked at the Rational Unified Process (RUP) or CMM/I methods and cringed at the learning curve and costs. • **you need to get software out the door without excuses.**

Ship It! A Practical Guide to Successful Software Projects
Jared Richardson and Will Gwaltney
(200 pages) ISBN: 0-9745140-4-7. $29.95
http://pragprog.com/titles/prj

Agile Practices

Agile Retrospectives

Mine the experience of your software development team continually throughout the life of the project. Rather than waiting until the end of the project—as with a traditional retrospective, when it's too late to help—agile retrospectives help you adjust to change *today*.

The tools and recipes in this book will help you uncover and solve hidden (and not-so-hidden) problems with your technology, your methodology, and those difficult "people issues" on your team.

Agile Retrospectives: Making Good Teams Great
Esther Derby and Diana Larsen
(170 pages) ISBN: 0-9776166-4-9. $29.95
http://pragprog.com/titles/dlret

Pragmatic Thinking and Learning

Software development happens in your head. Not in an editor, IDE, or design tool. In this book by Pragmatic Programmer Andy Hunt, you'll learn how our brains are wired, and how to take advantage of your brain's architecture. You'll master new tricks and tips to learn more, faster, and retain more of what you learn.

• Use the Dreyfus Model of Skill Acquisition to become more expert • Leverage the architecture of the brain to strengthen different thinking modes
• Avoid common "known bugs" in your mind
• Learn more deliberately and more effectively
• Manage knowledge more efficiently

**Pragmatic Thinking and Learning:
Refactor your Wetware**
Andy Hunt
(288 pages) ISBN: 978-1-9343560-5-0. $34.95
http://pragprog.com/titles/ahptl

Project Management

Manage It!

Manage It! is an award-winning, risk-based guide to making good decisions about how to plan and guide your projects. Author Johanna Rothman shows you how to beg, borrow, and steal from the best methodologies to fit your particular project. You'll find what works best for *you*.

• Learn all about different project lifecycles • See how to organize a project • Compare sample project dashboards • See how to staff a project • Know when you're done—and what that means.

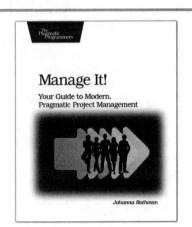

Manage It! Your Guide to Modern, Pragmatic Project Management
Johanna Rothman
(360 pages) ISBN: 0-9787392-4-8. $34.95
http://pragprog.com/titles/jrpm

Manage Your Project Portfolio

Too many projects? Want to organize them and evaluate them without getting buried under a mountain of statistics? You'll see how to determine the really important projects (which might not be what you think) as well as the projects you should *never* do. You'll learn how to tie your work to your organization's mission and show your board, your managers, and your staff what you can accomplish and when. You'll get a better view of the work you have, and learn how to make those difficult decisions, ensuring that all your strength is focused where it needs to be.

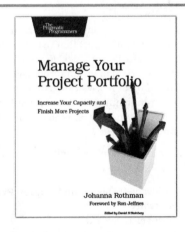

Manage Your Project Portfolio: Increase Your Capacity and Finish More Projects
Johanna Rothman
(200 pages) ISBN: 978-19343562-9-6. $32.95
http://pragprog.com/titles/jrport

Web Development

Design Accessible Web Sites

The 2000 U.S. Census revealed that 12% of the population is severely disabled. Sometime in the next two decades, one in five Americans will be older than 65. Section 508 of the Americans with Disabilities Act requires your website to provide *equivalent access* to all potential users. But beyond the law, it is both good manners and good business to make your site accessible to everyone. This book shows you how to design sites that excel for all audiences.

Design Accessible Web Sites: 36 Keys to Creating Content for All Audiences and Platforms
Jeremy Sydik
(304 pages) ISBN: 978-1-9343560-2-9. $34.95
http://pragprog.com/titles/jsaccess

Release It!

Whether it's in Java, .NET, or Ruby on Rails, getting your application ready to ship is only half the battle. Did you design your system to survive a sudden rush of visitors from Digg or Slashdot? Or an influx of real-world customers from 100 different countries? Are you ready for a world filled with flaky networks, tangled databases, and impatient users?

If you're a developer and don't want to be on call at 3 a.m. for the rest of your life, this book will help.

Release It! Design and Deploy Production-Ready Software
Michael T. Nygard
(368 pages) ISBN: 0-9787392-1-3. $34.95
http://pragprog.com/titles/mnee

Career Development

Land the Tech Job You Love

You've got the technical chops—the skills to get a great job doing what you love. Now it's time to get down to the business of planning your job search, focusing your time and attention on the job leads that matter, and interviewing to wow your boss-to-be.

You'll learn how to find the job you want that fits you and your employer. You'll uncover the hidden jobs that never make it into the classifieds or Monster. You'll start making and maintaining the connections that will drive your future career moves

You'll land the tech job you love.

Land the Tech Job You Love
Andy Lester
(225 pages) ISBN: 978-1934356-26-5. $23.95
http://pragprog.com/titles/algh

The Passionate Programmer

This book is about creating a remarkable career in software development. Remarkable careers don't come by chance. They require thought, intention, action, and a willingness to change course when you've made mistakes. Most of us have been stumbling around letting our careers take us where they may. It's time to take control.

This revised and updated second edition lays out a strategy for planning and creating a radically successful life in software development *(the first edition was released as My Job Went to India: 52 Ways To Save Your Job)*.

The Passionate Programmer: Creating a Remarkable Career in Software Development
Chad Fowler
(200 pages) ISBN: 978-1934356-34-0. $23.95
http://pragprog.com/titles/cfcar2

The Pragmatic Bookshelf

The Pragmatic Bookshelf features books written by developers for developers. The titles continue the well-known Pragmatic Programmer style and continue to garner awards and rave reviews. As development gets more and more difficult, the Pragmatic Programmers will be there with more titles and products to help you stay on top of your game.

Visit Us Online

Agile Coaching's Home Page
http://pragprog.com/titles/sdcoach
Source code from this book, errata, and other resources. Come give us feedback, too!

Register for Updates
http://pragprog.com/updates
Be notified when updates and new books become available.

Join the Community
http://pragprog.com/community
Read our weblogs, join our online discussions, participate in our mailing list, interact with our wiki, and benefit from the experience of other Pragmatic Programmers.

New and Noteworthy
http://pragprog.com/news
Check out the latest pragmatic developments, new titles and other offerings.

Save on the eBook

Save on the eBook versions of this title. Owning the paper version of this book entitles you to purchase the electronic versions at a terrific discount.

PDFs are great for carrying around on your laptop—they are hyperlinked, have color, and are fully searchable. Most titles are also available for the iPhone and iPod touch, Amazon Kindle, and other popular e-book readers.

Buy now at pragprog.com/coupon.

Contact Us

Online Orders: www.pragprog.com/catalog
Customer Service: support@pragprog.com
Non-English Versions: translations@pragprog.com
Pragmatic Teaching: academic@pragprog.com
Author Proposals: proposals@pragprog.com
Contact us: 1-800-699-PROG (+1 919 847 3884)